W9-DJN-634

It's Worth Your Life

It's Worth

A Christian Challenge

ASSOCIATION PRESS – NEW YORK

Your Life

To Youth Today

WITHDRAWN
by Unity Library

BY WILLIAM M. DYAL, JR.

UNITY SCHOOL LIBRARY
Unity Village
Lee's Summit, Missouri 64063

IT'S WORTH YOUR LIFE

Copyright © 1967 by
National Board of Young Men's Christian Associations

Association Press, 291 Broadway, New York, N.Y. 10007

All rights reserved, including the right of reproduction in whole or in part in any form, under the International, Pan-American, and Universal Copyright Conventions.

The quotations in this publication from the Revised Standard Version of the Bible, copyright 1946 and 1952 by the Division of Christian Education of the National Council of the Churches of Christ in the U.S.A., are used by permission.

Quotation from the poem, "Burnt Norton," from *Four Quartets,* by T. S. Eliot, copyright 1943, used by permission of Harcourt, Brace & World.

The poem, "The Day After Sunday," from *Times Three,* by Phyllis McGinley, originally appeared in the *New Yorker* magazine, copyright 1952 by Phyllis McGinley, reprinted by permission of The Viking Press, Inc.

The poem, "Talk," from *Selected Poems,* by Yevgeny Yevtushenko, copyright © 1962, used by permission of Penguin Books.

Quotations from the *Bible: A New Translation* by James Moffatt copyrighted 1954 by James Moffatt. Used by permission of Harper & Row, Publishers, Inc.

Quotations from *The New Testament in Modern English* by J. B. Phillips, copyright © 1958. Used by permission of The Macmillan Company.

Quotations from *The New English Bible, New Testament.* © The Delegates of the Oxford University Press and The Syndics of the Cambridge University Press 1961. Reprinted by permission.

"Prayer of Repentance," from *Are You Running With Me, Jesus?* by Malcolm Boyd. Copyright © 1965 by Malcolm Boyd. Reprinted by permission of Holt, Rinehart and Winston, Inc.

Quotations from *Markings,* by Dag Hammarskjöld, translated by Leif Sjoberg and W. H. Auden. © Copyright 1964 by Alfred A. Knopf, Inc. and Faber and Faber, Ltd. Reprinted by permission of Alfred A. Knopf, Inc.

Portion of a poem by Robert Anderson quoted by permission of *Saturday Review* and Cleveland Amory. From "First of the Month" column, *SR,* July 4, 1964.

Publisher's stock numbers: hardcover, 1638; paperback, 1642p
Library of Congress catalog card number: 67-14582

Printed in the United States of America

BV
4531.2
D98i

for EDIE
who loves life
and
shares hers
enthusiastically

Introduction

In many places, life is cheap. Warring Southeast Asian jungles, hungry Latin squatters' towns, African apartheid country, overcrowded big city ghettos, and racist-dominated towns all buy a man cheaply and look at his indignity or death with apathy.

The paradox is that Christian discipleship sees life as costly—worth the death of personal ambition, greed, or even the physical man. Consequently, individual Christians have through the ages identified with life as something valuable to be spent with purpose and passion.

Contemporary discipleship means to discern what God is doing now in the world, and to commit faith and life to the tasks and events which call for redemption. Discipleship is to witness by word and by act, in the spirit of Jesus Christ, to the costliness of life—and to let that witness be heard and seen in all the places where life is cheap.

Contents

CONTENTS

1

Is It Worth Your Life?

WHEN ASTRONAUT Edward White stepped into space for that famous first "space-walk," a world watched with excitement. Extensive research and preparation backed his adventure. Expensive rockets and scientific skill were employed. Literally thousands of people were involved. One singularly dramatic fact stands out, however. Astronaut White was pitting his own life against the conquest of space. To him, it was worth his life.

IDEALISM IS "IN"

In an age of restlessness and changing values, a new idealism may be being born. It is definitely "in" to ask whether a career is worth one's life. It is not "kookie" to want to be and do more than just make a living. An article on American idealism in the mid-sixties put it this way: "In the 1920's and 1930's, those among the young who were alienated from middle class white America went to Europe to write, to paint, to compose, to study, to fight, to be free from an America they had come to condemn for its cultural and social impurities. In the 1960's the young go to Africa, Asia, or Latin

America for the Peace Corps, they teach in Mississippi, demonstrate in Alabama, tutor in Chicago slums. They do the work they are doing, not in support of an abstract idea, but for the sake of the people they are able to help."*

Today a successful man may still be unhappy with the meaning of his life. The affluent may be uneasy with his wealth. Freedom is a byword of the day. Freedom is a clarion call for personal involvement both at home and abroad. Freedom also is responsibility. In an exciting and demanding age, who wants to settle for boredom? Who wants to settle for mere self-serving or special-interest-serving? Who dares settle for the get-by disposition or the mediocre standard?

CHANGE IS EVERYWHERE

It is true that even though your body may live out the years allotted it, the heart of youth can die and the mind close tight. Non-commitment is a leukemia which will sap your vitality. But what a way to face an exciting age! Where lies adventure today? Adventure is change, for one thing.

Change is accelerating about you. There has been and will be more substantial change in your lifetime than in all previous history put together. A revolutionary earthquake is changing the once familiar landscape of national boundaries, forms of government, educational methods, social groupings, methods of production, and ecclesiastical forms. It is not easy to learn to live on this new land, especially when the earthquake continues to destroy even some of the new forms before one has discovered how to adapt to them.

Out of nowhere have come experts who move easily in a realm of thought and practice that most of us cannot understand. In a short span they have accomplished what the most

*For the source of this and other quotes, please see References at the end of the book.

extravagant follower of Jules Verne would not have imagined. From deep sea to distant moon, man is on the move. He believes he can create life in a test tube, extend man's years, and learn to control the elements. He builds faster vehicles, constructs more elaborate highways, taller buildings. His new machines banish his ancient toil, his computers outthink him.

Who wouldn't like to be a part of such an expanding universe? Your day is new and different. You will live it on new terms, not according to the dictates of father or grandfather. The errors of older generations plague you—and they should.

Jules Feiffer bluntly pictures the dilemma in a cartoon. A portly gentleman is addressing a sign-carrying youth: "I'll tell you what really bothers you kids today: YOU JUST DON'T WANT TO GROW UP!" The youth replies: "I once wanted to grow up, but then I took a look at the grown-ups around me—complaining about the jobs they hate and dying of boredom months after they retire from them. Picking wives out of the girls they are not attracted to and remaining attracted to girls who they think are tramps. Watching TV six nights a week so they don't have to talk to the family. Joining a club one night a week so they can talk to the boys. Preaching to their kids about their inalienable rights, and when the kids try to exercise a few, warning them to GROW UP. Mister, to my generation, NOT wanting to grow up is a sign of maturity."

Feiffer's "tongue-in-cheekness" is well taken. New scenes require new wisdom, new demands, new courage. Hypocrisy is to be shunned. Youth want to go where the action is. They often trip over the unfulfilled good intentions of their elders, however. Dialogue between generations is too infrequent. Bumbling youthful amateurs need the counsel of knowledgeable professionals. But the old "pros" also need new blood.

Too many of today's idealistic high schoolers and collegians become tomorrow's tired and cautious cynics.

Change is everywhere. For the first time in the history of any nation, there is the possibility in our own to banish from our borders the age-old cripplers of nature: hunger, disease, poverty, and ignorance. Wealth and know-how and even government support cannot bring it to pass, however. The brilliance of youth, vitality of creative minds and bodies, and commitment under God to one's fellowman are required. Service of fellowman and care of fellowman are moral necessities. Love must replace "gross personal product" as your supreme value. Your body, mind, and spirit can be God's tools for making sense of this accelerated change.

"Has anything more wonderful ever happened in history? We are tearing the old skin off mankind and giving it a new one. That is not an occupation for people with weak nerves." So Arthur Koestler has the character Ivanov say in *Darkness at Noon.* Economic, social, and political revolution sweeps the world. Old structures are giving way to new, and new nations are emerging. Radical social change in customs and cultures is occurring.

In just such radical occupation you can be employed. Your life is already jam up against class stratification, racial discrimination, power politics, and economic determinism. Urgent tasks surround you. Hundreds of thousands of unemployed men are chronic burdens to themselves and society. Segregation and discrimination still represent a major pattern of life. The inner cities are filthy, corrupt, and stricken with disease next door to affluence, beauty, and health. War continues to bite off a giant hunk of the federal budget and, more importantly, the nation's manpower. Developing nations of the world beg for that same manpower, in education, engineering, and community development.

Dare you invest your life in such radical vocation? The biblical word is plain: "So we are ambassadors for Christ, God making his appeal through us" (2 Cor. 5:20 RSV). This cuts through to boldness, to concern. This calls for preparation and a responsive life. Do you have what it takes?

FRONTIERS FOR ACTION

In today's churches we have often sought to find a more comfortable condition than the Christ—and his destiny, the cross. For the cross readily reveals what happens when prejudice, hate, provincialism, and traditionalism clash with reconciling love. The church must be willing to be on the ground for that clash to take place while at the same time serving as the ambassador of healing.

Authentic ministry will belong to the church only as she confronts the major ethical and moral frontiers of the day. They are complex! Oversimplified pious answers and categorical programs will not suffice. Man, major issues, the nations, and the future are all at stake. These contemporary frontiers demand the best the church has in brain and spirit power and life commitment. That may mean you!

Materialism

One such frontier for your action is *the tyranny of things.* We live in an age of superabundance. The orgy of goods dulls our sensitivities. Faith is exchanged for information, programs, and security. *Newsweek* described the "Good Non-Life" as a time of ultimate miracle products giving "indulgence without penalties, experience without risk, deprivation without deprival. Gluttony can now be non-fattening, lust can be non-procreative, and even thought can be reduced to a complex of magnetic tapes, transistors and computer cards."

"Love things and use people" is a way of life representing a complete upheaval in values. We are serious about trivialities (hairdos, electric toothbrushes, and what have you) but trivial about reality. Property values assume more importance than human worth and fulfillment. And the result is complacency toward finding Christian solutions of burning social issues.

In a materialistic tyranny, not only individuals, but churches and denominations can be victimized. Economic determinism is a powerful force. Personal security, church solvency, and denominational growth are prevalent motivating forces. Numbers assume importance beyond the true worth of things. Buildings and institutions mushroom. It is easy to be a pessimist about money and mortar, however. Inside brick walls you need fire and courage, talent and purpose, sweat and self-criticism.

Greed and selfish ambition can twist a young life. Loss of perspective scuttles principles and moral courage. Creativity can be dimmed in the pursuit of wealth or power.

Sex

A second frontier can be described as *the enthronement of eros*. Weaned on *Playboy* and a happiness kick which says, "Have fun," ours is a time of moral rebellion camouflaged by social graces. Contrived sexuality is the guideline of the day. Professor Robert Fitch calls the problem a "sexplosion" and blisters our orgy of open-mindedness.

Christianity seems tongue-tied in the face of the growth of teen marriages, the tripling in twenty years of births out of wedlock, and the proliferation of divorce, marriage becoming more and more mere serial polygamy. This moral frontier begs for deeper Christian insight and love. Man has been insulted by being considered more an appetite than an intellect. He is approached as a body rather than as a person. Television commercials and magazine ads seek to lure consumers by subtly injecting sex. The consumer's passions and emotions are cunningly manipulated. In such a context, the Christian experience is called "treasure in earthen vessels."

Man as "earthen vessel" never faced life more complex nor temptation more attractive. The invitations abound to "taste," "sample," "experiment," and to ignore the consequences.

Subversion of Power and Knowledge

A third frontier for discipleship is *the subversion of power and knowledge*. The knowledge of God and of his will for man has been debased and channeled to secondary ends or even to evil ends. The Scriptures teach that "the earth is the Lord's and the fullness thereof." But our generation is saying: "The world is my oyster." The gospel calls for shared wealth, for genuine concern for human need. But the current attitude is: "After all, we're *not* Santa Claus."

Economic strength and political power have tended to build a superiority complex among Americans. Both in nationalism and in religion we are guilty of trying to be the Messiah rather than to proclaim Messiah's dominion. Even overseas missionary motivation is sometimes erroneously linked to keeping the United States safe from war. God is expected to perform wonders for American well-being. Charles West aptly reminds us, however, that God is not an actor in our drama, but we are actors in his. He is not a character in our history, but we are characters in his.

A high school senior often discussed the world news with his buddies. No matter how serious the events, one of them always replied, "So what, we'll be okay. God's on his throne." One day, the senior replied, "You may be right—but don't forget that that throne *is not* located in Washington, D.C.!"

Nowhere is the subversion of power and knowledge more evident than in the ethical dilemma of nuclear power. The issue is emotion-charged. Rather than recognizing the awesome burden of responsibility for mankind, we too easily resort to national pride or hysterical fear. Civics classes and patriotism are too often taught by rote. Emotional spine tingling about flags and parades is no substitute for the self-discipline democracy demands. What is pride? To have the distinction of being earth's last generation of men? What greater subversion of power can there be!

We have become preoccupied in fighting communism with bombs and with dollars, rather than with ideas of revolution, of freedom, of justice. The dynamic vocabulary of the Christian gospel has been preempted by the world's non-Christians. At the same time, the church's vocabulary has often been subverted by pettiness and prejudice to sound a regional, national, political, or racial party line.

The power of many great religious communities is too easily poured into the task of searching for the least common denominator rather than of seeking to be prophetic. A sermon or an activity or program thus is projected only if it will be acceptable to the majority. In crowd pleasing, neither God nor man is served. Power and knowledge represent for religion a formidable ethical frontier. The church cannot survive the subversion of that power for petty ends. Neither can you, personally.

The church is in the midst of life to remind her own and the whole world that God transcends all human systems. All are under his judgment. The church bears witness to a gospel which proclaims the outgoing love of God for every man—

regardless of nation, race, tongue, or political allegiance. God is the God not just of the Democrats, but also of the Republicans. God is the God not just of whites, but also of blacks. God is the God not just of New York, but also of Oklahoma. God is the God not just of the United States, but also of Russia, and Nigeria, and . . .

This message must not be subverted or compromised.

Man's Alienation

A fourth ethical frontier which you confront is *the alienation of man*. He is a lost soul. He becomes rebel to God, rebel to self, and rebel to his fellowman. Contemporary writers have described his plight. One writes of man "shut up to solitary confinement inside his own skin." T. S. Eliot described "Men and bits of paper, whirled by the cold wind." Erich Fromm talks of the "triumph of the faceless," of man lost in the crowd. And to borrow a plaintive line from a Broadway hit song: "People who need people are the luckiest people in the world."

But the ad writers get at man's alienation even more eloquently. Man is approached en masse as a body, a consumer, a producer, a mind, a passenger, a voter, and—for benefit of the churches—a prospect!

What barriers must be tumbled for you to see man as man! He is captive of his own mobility, caught in the new nomad way of American life. Or he is victimized by blind tribal emotions, seen only as a migrant, or poor white trash, or country club, or Jew, or Negro, or "nigger."

WHAT THE CHURCH (YOU) CAN DO

The New Testament describes Christianity in unique terms. Where is the "Church of the Cup of Cold Water" today? Can alcoholics not be healed in the name of Christ? Must the dope addict be left to the back alleys? Where else can the teen-age unwed mother go? Is the church no haven for people on the run? No solace for the mentally ill? No guide for the intellectual seeker? No counsel for the lonely city dweller? No warmth for the forgotten aging? No encouragement for the school dropout? No acceptance for the rebel? No concern for the student from another nation? No fellowship for the racial minority member?

Jesus' words are jolting: "Whoever welcomes you, welcomes me; and whoever welcomes me is welcoming the one who sent me" (Matt. 10:40 Phillips). These are ominous words for one who would police the altar of God or establish a "Checkpoint Charlie" at the church's door. "Checkpoint Charlie" may belong to the Berlin Wall but not to the church. Christ welcomed persons from every condition of life.

The church (and you) is at these frontiers and a hundred more where men have need. Renewal for the church and salvation for men are involved. This encounter between the church and society is fraught with grave problems, but also characterized by exciting possibilities for your discipleship.

New meaning must be pumped into dried-up biblical wordwells, such as "salt," "light," "yeast," and "ambassador." The concept of the "gathered" church must be dramatically stretched to many more locations than one. The church in the apartment building, the church in the hotel, the church in the plant, the church in the hospital, the church in the tenement, the church in the resort—these are all new opportunities for worship and evangelism. Man must be ministered to where he is, not just where we wish him to be.

Congregational resources will be taxed to meet the staggering needs. Lay training and ministry is urgent. Spectator worship is out. Pulpit to pew needs to be a two-way street rather than a dead end. Congregations want to talk back.

But face facts! Confrontation with social change is never easy. All the grace the church can muster will be needed to keep from being bought out. It would be simpler to look the other way—simpler yet to salute the status quo—simplest of all to sell out and call it the will of God.

Simple—that is, if Jesus' prayer were not so relevant: "I have given them thy word; and the world has hated them because they are not of the world, even as I am not of the world. I do not pray that thou shouldst take them out of the world, but that thou shouldst keep them from the evil one. They are not of the world, even as I am not of the world. Sanctify them in the truth; thy word is truth. As thou didst send me into the world, so I have sent them into the world. And for their sake I consecrate myself, that they also may be consecrated in truth.

"I do not pray for these only, but also for those who are to believe in me through their word, that they may all be one; even as thou, Father, art in me, and I in thee, that they also may be in us, so that the world may believe that thou hast sent me" (John 17:14-21 RSV).

WHAT'S IT WORTH TO YOU?

Is it worth *your* life to get involved? Few thrills can equal the discovery of purpose for life. The Christian is called to pilgrimage. The pilgrimage begins with genuine zest for life. Gratitude to God for the gift of life is the starting point for making sense of one's life. Committed enthusiasm cuts through dull tedium and restlessness. Zest for the Christian life refuses to join the cult of mediocrity, resists the trap of a vacuum of values. Even the commonplace is transformed, and both men and things seem to brim with meaning. Christian salvation is a radical awakening to a vital and throbbing world. A sense of adventure is born. The hungry hearts and itching minds of other men challenge your very life.

Christian vocation was never intended to so sterilize the mind and spirit that the drama of man, his grandeur and his misery, would be hidden from you. On the contrary, genuine Christian faith opens up life . . . and asks you what you will be as a contemporary man. The answer may change the course of your life.

Not everyone will go along with you. Some will mock; some will laugh. The ambitious may think you are "off your rocker." Idealistic naïve fervor on one hand and jaded cynicism on the other are seen all about you. There are old fogies and young fogies. Chronological age is not the only dividing line, however. Dr. John Buettner Janusch of Duke University, prior to beginning a long-term study of apes and monkeys, said: "I enjoy working with baboons and lemurs because the baboons remind me of my colleagues on university faculties and the lemurs remind me of undergraduates. Lemurs are bright-eyed, bushy-tailed and can't believe the world is the way it is. Baboons, on the other hand, are intelligent, sociable, clever, untidy and you can't trust them." You may not be able to characterize the people around you quite as succinctly as this professor, but your contemporaries are going to react to you in many ways.

Nevertheless, today is yours. Every age has witnessed the power of youth. Alexander the Great was but a boy when his reign began. Joan of Arc died at age nineteen. William Pitt was England's Prime Minister at age twenty-two. John Kennedy had been Congressman, Senator, and President by age forty-four. Age is not a major factor. Vitality and commitment are.

"Who Am I?"

This modern-day pilgrimage, begun with a sense of enthusiastic adventure, inevitably leads you to a quest for the meaning of your life. "Who am I?" and "What is my life?" are the basic questions. Do not ask them, however, unless you want your own private "boat" rocked.

You ask "Who am I?" in a technical and automated age. You can easily begin to feel computerized. Or you can sense being lost in the crowd and anonymity. God plays no game of hide and seek. He calls man by name to be the person he was created and redeemed to be.

When this happens for you, you see your faults and your blind spots. You begin honestly to accept and weigh your virtues and your strengths. You inventory your preparation and what more is needed. You take a hard look at your talents. You evaluate your sensitivity (or lack of it) to persons and to human need. You cross-examine the attempts to brainwash you into believing that material security is the ultimate motivation, that compassionate concern is sissy, that morality is relative, or that faith is excess baggage.

Your pilgrimage to discover the meaning of your life brings you face to face with what you now are and with what you can become.

A Whole Person

Integrity, or wholeness, can result. When you attempt to make faith and action jibe, you are on the way. The worth of life is tied up with truth, with being a whole person. Wholeness means all you are, have been, and hope to be. God wants a man's whole life, "not just his job or his prayers or his money. . . . All our choices—work, play, marriage, politics, reading, speaking—all are part of our long conversation with God," wrote Stephen F. Bayne. Private thoughts and public performance are harmonious. Resolutions made in worship find outlet in daily living. Prayer is born of real experience.

Wholeness means that life is not compartmentalized. Home is not one compartment, church another, job another, school another. There are no watertight partitions between the areas of your life. The mainstream of purpose pours through each, bringing harmony and significance. Each area of life enriches the others. They are related. You can forget the pretense of playing different roles in the compartments of your life. You are becoming a whole person, the same person.

As a whole person you become passionately concerned about the wholeness of others. The worth and dignity of man come alive for you in the persons of poor and rich alike, white and black, American and foreigner. People become for you "thous" instead of "its." In other words, you respect them as persons and do not treat them as objects. You know you can never again be content to be aloof or dispassionate. You make a contract with life itself, in the spirit of Christ.

As a Christian of integrity you dare to ask "Why?" about the issues of the day: immorality (private and corporate), poverty, injustice, war, segregation, and power politics. You commit yourself to be an innovator, a pioneer, or an iconoclast if necessary. You dare to see through tradition and superficial image to the truth of things. You recognize the obsolescence in ideas: the resistance to a world outlook, the inability to understand human need, and the human lag in a scientific age which has outdistanced man's spirit. You dare to believe that nothing anyone is doing makes sense unless it is connected to the making of peace with justice.

Where Are You Needed?

Now a new level of self-questioning begins to take place. "Where am I needed most?" Jesus' fulfillment of Isaiah's words become your call:

"The Spirit of the Lord is upon me,

because he has anointed me to preach good news to the
   poor.
He has sent me to proclaim release to the captives
and recovering of sight to the blind,
to set at liberty those who are oppressed,
to proclaim the acceptable year of the Lord" (Luke 4:18–
   19 RSV).

Others of Christ's words also become very personal and
pointed: ". . . for I was hungry and you gave me food, I was
thirsty and you gave me drink, I was a stranger and you welcomed me, I was naked and you clothed me, I was sick and
you visited me, I was in prison and you came to me . . . as
you did it to one of the least of these my brethren, you did it
to me" (Matt. 25:35–36, 40 RSV).

    The scope, location, and name of your career become spe-
cific and important. More than just a job is involved. Faith
and life are poured into the answer to the question, "Is it
worth my life?" Costly education, personal morality, disci-
pline, experience, repentance and forgiveness, Christian
growth and love are all poured into the vessel of your vocation. You submit to hard, intellectual study on the one hand
and to dirty, practical work on the other. Certificates and
degrees will be necessary. But even these are qualifications
that fade and have less value the farther away from them one
gets. Consequently, in this rapidly shifting world, preparation never ceases.

    The career may bear the label of the church, or it may not.
The career may be in your home country, or foreign. It may
be social work, or teaching, or homemaking. It may be
preaching, or medicine, or engineering. It may be farming,
or biology, or space exploration.

    Extraordinarily good diagnosticians are needed—trained

minds that can sense change before it happens. Statesmen are required to determine which piece of society's unfinished business needs attention first and to help the nation take the leap. Where armies now move, healers and teachers will soon be needed. Where provincialism and prejudice have held sway, bridge builders between men will be required to help spell out the terms of economic and social justice. Men of peace and goodwill are demanded for the tasks of legislation, scientific research, and diplomacy. In the competitive world of business, men of integrity must challenge shoddy business ethics. On the restless university scene, realistic Christian professors will have to lead their students on a creative search for truth. Pastors who speak and live courageously and relevantly will have to guide their congregations to understand how to live in a new day. Christians who recognize God as Creator of every man will be called to the risky world of automation to remind the times that man is man and not a machine, that the machine is to serve man and not man the machine.

Sensitive sociologists and psychologists are needed to reach and help the outcasts whose dreams are dead. Depending on social position, they are the people acting in damaging ways: crime, delinquency, narcotics, sexual insecurity, cheating, suicide. Often they are members of ethnic minorities. The strain upon them comes from living with what they cannot accept but cannot change.

Your pilgrimage will also stretch your world. Towns and counties will grow to include nations and continents. Your ears will prick up to the sounds of other lands. Your tongue will long to speak more than English. Gandhi's words, carved on the facade of India's pavilion at the 1964–65 New York World's Fair, will strike a response in you: "I do not want my house to be walled in on all sides and my windows to be stuffed. I want the cultures of all lands to be blown about my house as freely as possible. ...." You will recognize that the revolution that moves like a tidal wave across other nations once washed our shores and does now again.

REVOLUTION

Revolution is a key description of your world. Emergency has ceased to be emergency and become chronic distress. Poverty, ignorance, disease and tyranny ride roughshod like four modern horsemen of the apocalypse. New nations leave their launching pads in a constant Cape Kennedy-type countdown. The gamble is whether they will orbit or not. The revolutions of equality, vast technical and material change, and population explosion are matched only by the aspiration explosion. In Latin America, Asia, and Africa, the disinherited are demanding voice and vote. Strong winds of economic, political, and social innovation are sweeping nations.

Beneath the turmoil, however, there is a vast inertia, a great ocean of people and tradition, slow to respond to the storm at the surface, yet moving with powerful currents which will soon be felt at the top. These people want material benefits. But also, they want to find justice, dignity, and individual worth. These we Americans have professed but found difficult to share.

National boundaries mean less and less today. Native tongue only leaves one speechless in the larger world. Culture shock is an experience more and more common. To ask "Where am I needed most?" may well lead you far beyond your own land. The new age is more equalitarian and fraternal, less paternal and hierarchical. A new magazine launched some time ago in Europe has many millions of subscribers. Its title, *Nous, les copains,* comes from an old slang word referring originally to those who shared the same bread. It is a synonym for "companion." It is also a theme for your life.

Regardless of label or geography or job description, the new age demands committed Christians who can affirm "It is worth my life!"

Chapter

2

Key to the Authentic: Truth

A STUDENT WAITED for me following a lecture. His question was straight to the point: "Is it right to keep my faith when my mind says it's a fake?"

His question is a leading one. Where is the truly authentic to be found? Obviously no one wants to commit his life knowingly to that which may be quackery. Faith which is a fake is not faith.

THE CHRISTIAN: A SEEKER OF TRUTH

Without apology Christian discipleship engages you in a search for truth. Secure faith rests upon an integration of rational belief with emotional commitment. Faith and reason are not divisive or intended to be competitive. They represent two different capacities within a man. Insofar as they compete with each other within a man, he is confused and at war within himself. Jesus said, "You shall love the Lord your God with all your heart, and with all your soul, and with all your mind" (Matt. 22:37 RSV). The whole man is called into discipleship. When a man is asked to love God with his heart he is also asked to love God with his mind. To do otherwise is to divide man into two domains. In some religious circles such division is commonly practiced. Commitment to the truth of God and the truth about self, however, never divides a man so that he finds himself torn and confused. He is not two men but truly one.

Sir Walter Raleigh said that there is no mistress or guide who has led her followers and servants into greater miseries than truth. Truth is a hard taskmaster. The pilgrimage for truth is not a pleasure excursion. Nor is it an elusive search for the never-to-be-found "holy grail." It is the struggle to be open to light and understanding, which can break through to us even in the midst of rebellion and fear:

ENEMIES OF TRUTH

We fear confrontation with truth because revelation can be painful. Defensively we react to protect our prior point of view. We hasten to find arguments to support what we already believe rather than to seek truth which will overwhelm anything we have yet conceived. We fear to see the shallow quality of what we believe and the superficial nature of our understanding.

Leave us undisturbed by truth long enough and we tend to build a case for half-truths that make them seem ordained by God, simply because they are familiar.

Reactionism

It is more comfortable to stick by yesterday's opinions than to be subjected to the stimulus of today's thought. Consequently we subject today's facts to a prefabricated set of opinions. The conclusions are built in and thus are not genuine conclusions based on truth. To enshrine yesterday's ideas may paralyze today's new insights.

Childhood religious understanding must mature. William

Temple explained: "The child accepts what he is told concerning God as he accepts all else that he is told by those in trust upon whom he lives, according to his capacity to receive it. In the same way he accepts the dogmatic assertion that $7 \times 7 = 49$ without working it out for himself. But in most departments of life the basis of belief is gradually shifted from the authority of parents and teachers to his own experience and his own reflection upon this. And so far as this happens, his belief becomes more autonomous. It is his own; he has verified and vindicated it."

Truth on a Time Schedule

The pilgrimage for truth is thwarted also when one attempts to choose his own time schedule for the breakthrough of truth. A novelist has a character say, "I would rather think about that tomorrow." A kind of mental hearing aid is turned on or off as it is convenient, to shut out for the moment that which one does not want to hear, lest he begin to believe it.

Extremism

Especially widespread today is an extremist reaction to truth. Large-scale organizations thrive on the unwillingness to face facts. Countless sincere people are involved, and have given their allegiance to these groups. The John Birch Society and many of the professional anti-Communist organizations often represent a distortion of truth about our world and its movements.

Such extremism is a reaction against the threat of change. Extremists are engaged in over-response to new facts and new possibilities for man and society. They thrive on high emotionalism closely wed to authoritarianism. They are cultists in that they are uncritical of themselves and look instead for scapegoats among the "enemy." False intellectualism dominates them. It may be either an anti-intellectual spirit or a pseudo-intellectual approach. The extremist is sometimes motivated by a highly commercialized self-interest.

Any scheme, or organization, or leader, or institution, or church group which insists on keeping you from all the facts is a threat to your pilgrimage toward truth. In effect they say to you that their partial understanding is absolute. Any deviation from their pronounced "absolute" is an offense, a crime, or a sin, depending on the nature of the group.

Clichés

Clichés are also enemies of truth. Vitality is poured down the drain of stale triteness, of shopworn religious phrases. So much preaching and religious conversation tends to be meaningless mumbo-jumbo. Eugene Nida rightly calls it "Protestant Latin." But clichés are inadequate when you are in the midst of crises. When you face the death of a loved one, prayer and dirt sprinkled over the grave are not enough. When you have succumbed to sexual temptation, remembering how to pronounce *"agape"* as the Greek word for love seems useless. When your business has failed and you are on the brink of economic disaster, ethical abstractions are senseless.

In such hours man is up against the cold facts of life. When he wrestles with these ultimate problems, he is in truth a theologian under God. For this reason, David Edwards points out that the new breed of radical theologians ". . . have themselves said that the theology which is most needed must come mainly from laymen. If it is true that Christian doctrine needs to be revitalized by immersion and experience in reality, then it is surely also true that a social worker, or a housewife, or a commercial traveler, is likely to be at least as useful as a parson in coming up with the right material. The call to be in some sense a theologian will alarm many a layman. . . .

But this call must be heard if the Christian message is ever to be restated in language understood by our secularized century."

Consequently, questions about God, man, society, family, sex, and all the rest have to be stated in realistic terms. The whole theological conversation has to be cast in terms of contemporary situations and relationships: white-Negro, segregationist-integrationist, Protestant-Catholic-Jew, Anglo American-Latin American, Jew-Arab, labor-management, Republican-Democrat, male-female, have-have not, egghead-illiterate. This is where we live. Here is where truth must be sought, found, and followed.

THE DILEMMA OF THE TRUTH SEEKER

I find myself often asking Kant's three questions: What can I know? What ought I to do? What can I hope? I ask these questions and many other related ones in a fantastically pluralistic society. The variety of answers offered is a nightmarish supermarket of ideas.

Truth Seeking in the Space Age

The bewilderment is increased because of the Space Age. The Soviet cosmonaut Titov reported that God was not visible from his space rocket window. Obviously not! However, his smug word only points up the longtime bewilderment with which many face the traditional and literal accounts of a two-story universe building with earth on the main floor, heaven upstairs, and hell in the cellar. The whole framework is shattered in the knowledge of the billions of other worlds in God's creation. But the Psalmist gives help in this bewilderment:

"When I look at thy heavens, the work of thy fingers,
the moon and the stars which thou hast established;
what is man that thou art mindful of him,

and the son of man that thou dost care for him?
Yet thou hast made him little less than God,
   and dost crown him with glory and honor.
Thou hast given him dominion over the works of thy hands;
   thou hast put all things under his feet . . ." (Ps. 8:3-6
RSV).

As with the Psalmist, we are not so confounded with the God
of space as with the God of life. Yet, we know God revealed
in Jesus Christ, as man. Georgia Harkness reminds us, "Jesus
is not our only avenue to the discovery of God. As we have
seen, in the beauty and bounty and orderliness of nature, in
the best of human insights and strivings of the ages, in the
upward climb of man and even in the thwarting of human
desire that abruptly halts our course when we sin against
God, are revelations of the Eternal. But gleaming high above
all is the manifestation of God in human life that Jesus Christ
presents. When we see Jesus, we know what God is and what
he requires of us."

Our God Is "Too Small"

Why is belief so difficult then? Is it because God is re-
stricted to the history of the Bible? Is he God only of Abra-
ham and Isaac and Paul? Is he not also the God of today's
John Browns and Mary Smiths? Indeed there are problems
in the living God. Although man is never without knowledge
of God, he is basically ignorant of God. He is separated from
God because he produces distorted images of God and
adores those images! Here then is our problem: The images
of God, his many names and faces, so distort reality that we
cannot believe. Phyllis McGinley's poetic insight is particularly apropos:

Always on Monday, God's in the morning papers
His name is a headline, His works are rumored abroad.

Having been praised by men who are movers and
   shapers,
From prominent pulpits, newsworthy is God.

On page twenty-seven, just opposite fashion trends,
One reads at a glance how he scolded the Baptists.
Was firm with the Catholics, practical with the Friends,
To Unitarians pleasantly non-committal.

In print are his numerous aspects, too: God smiling,
God vexed, God thunderous, God whose mansions are
   pearl,
Political God, God frugal, God reconciling Himself
   with science,
God guiding the Campfire Girls.

Always on Monday morning the press reports
God as revealed to His vicars in various guises—
Benevolent, stormy, patient, or out of sorts.
God knows which God is the God God recognizes.

God is conveniently described in terms of special projects,
particular churches, pet peeves, and national ideals. To see
him thus is to have him a provincial prisoner, in our minds
at least.

God brooks no such idolatrous images nor rivals, however. Whenever God is imprisoned in provincialisms and
prejudice, truth is distorted. Some time ago there came to my
desk a pamphlet entitled "God the First Segregationist." In
such concepts God is hopelessly distorted. Truth is impaired.
The pilgrimage for truth is betrayed. At other times the truth
of God is distorted when he is given an American passport
and assigned attributes of American culture. Neither a white
face nor a Southern or Yankee accent nor a role as the
"Great White Father of the American Way of Life" can

capture God. It is easy to understand why other nations have often found it difficult to understand the true God when we have so often described him as an American appendage.

We Distort Christ Too

Similar distortions of truth occur in our teachings and approaches to Christ. "Let us renounce the well-behaved Jesus innocent of scandal and controversy; the Jesus of superstition memorialized in dashboard statuettes and lucky charms; the fanciful, ineffectual, effeminate, effete Jesus of the cinema whom the multitudes found irresistibly attractive; the soft, spiritual, sentimental Jesus of Salman and other vulgar caricatures; the farsighted Jesus teaching democracy to primitive people centuries before the French and American revolutions; the imaginary Jesus thought to be an unfortunate victim of a gross violation of due process of law. . . . Let us, in the name of Christian orthodoxy, expose and repudiate the fairy-tale Jesus of Sunday-school story books; the ridiculous Jesus fashioned after the manner of the white Anglo-Saxon Protestant; the unapproachable Jesus captive in tabernacles; the shiny, fragrant Jesus of snow-white raiment unspoiled by sweat or blood or the smell of fish; the religiose Jesus, an ascetic too esoteric for this world." William Stringfellow's biting words here vividly point up the heavy-handed distortion surrounding the person of Christ. Such distortions have clouded truth and made faith difficult. The underbrush of tradition and fantasy must be cleared away.

It All Happens in "Real Life"

At the same time, truth does not come through cold, calculating search. To profess Christ as one's Lord is not a matter of trying to ascertain by wit only what is true or false about him. A Christian confession of faith is made in real life, in concrete situations. Your faith is what you live for. It is commitment and continuous action involving everything that you are, including knowing, feeling, willing, and acting.

Georgia Harkness once again offers insight: "It is faith that enables us to have eyes to see and ears to hear. It is faith as 'insight' that quickens the mind to truer 'sight.' As one learns the truth about science only when his eyes are opened by an eagerness that drives him to learn, as one really sees great art or listens to great music only when his soul is sensitive to it, as one finds depths of richness in a friend only through an outgoingness of spirit that opens new channels, so one learns the truth about God only when he 'stands in faith.' One may get a detached sort of knowledge, which is true enough as far as it goes, by a weighing of arguments and canvassing of evidence as to the existence and nature of God. One does not really get to Christian faith until he lets God capture his spirit."

What brings insight into Scripture, religious symbols, and theological arguments is the Christian faith of the interpreter, at grips with the contemporary. Faith is not born in an ivory tower or in sheltered piety. Rather, faith is verbalized out of the seeker's wrestling with human situations. The serious seeker recognizes how much is at stake. He is open and responsive. He avoids flippant questions and garbled responses. He keeps on asking, "What has this to do with me?"

The primary claim of the Christian gospel then is radical awakening. "Ye must be born again"; " . . . and their eyes were opened" are expressions often used in the New Testament. A man comes alive. He begins to care deeply about his own existence and the meaning of existence. This radical awakening to the truth of life as found in Christ is closely related to commitment to living that truth. Paul Tillich has written: "In Christianity truth is found if it is done, and done if it is found. . . . The decision for or against truth is *the* life and death decision, and this decision is identical with the decision in which Christ is accepted or rejected. You cannot have opinion about the Christ after you have faced him. You can only do the truth by following him, or do the lie by denying him." Thus there is no cleavage between theory and practice, between belief and commitment. Truth is saving truth. To acknowledge the lordship of Christ is to be willing to live by its claims.

DOUBT IS NECESSARY

Having said all this, you may be thinking, "Where is there any room for doubt?" The answer is: There is more than just *room* for doubt; doubt is necessary to faith. It is not sinful to doubt. The real sin comes with bland, unthinking acceptance which pretends to be sure when one is not sure at all. Nor do we deal with doubts by ignoring them. Nor have we dealt with them when we have only repressed them. To repress them is simply to drive them into the recesses of our subconscious minds. There they seem to gather strength and erupt eventually in cynicism.

The capacity to doubt is one of man's genuine powers. Many great men have ushered in truth when in the face of a universally accepted falsehood they have dared to assert, "I doubt that!" Frankly, some of our churches and theologies have been saved from some of their worst falsehoods by such daring persons.

When a spirit of anti-intellectualism prevails, one tends to squelch his doubts. "No Trespassing" signs posted in religious life indicate that clear thinking and full expression of one's doubts and convictions are not welcome. In such a climate young people become fearful about expressing their doubts openly lest they be rebuked. Some ministers tend to stifle authentic questions, even from the pulpit, for fear of being accused of heresy. Rebellion is fomented in the person who has had to keep his questions in check.

There is no room in the life of the modern church for such a negative atmosphere. Adequate dialogue between preacher and pew, parent and child, theologian and lay Christian is urgently needed. The church does not have to defend God as an overprotective parent might seek to defend his child. God is not the child of the church. Truth walks with bold steps. It needs no bodyguard. Truth is not the enemy of intellectual freedom and vigor of mind, but rather the friend.

At times, however, doubt may arise out of moral evasion. Doubt can be a smoke screen seeking to cover up basic immorality. At other times, physical illness, emotional fatigue, loneliness, or rejection provide a climate in which doubt breeds and grows. When these situations are resolved, doubt may more easily be routed. Surrounding yourself only with negative people who are professional doubters is not the answer either. One who seeks truth seeks counsel and help wherever he can find it.

A spirit of adventure is characteristic of the search for truth. Hard fact is to be encountered. But there is also mystery. Without this sense of mystery related to the "incomparables" and the "unfathomables" of Christian faith, the air would be too thin to breathe. Adventure is not finicky about what it finds or about what is involved in the finding. The search for truth must be regarded as primary; avoidance of error must be secondary. Truth must take its chances. If you fear you might stumble on evidence disproving your preconceived notions, the adventure of truth is already a shambles.

The man of faith then is one who grapples honestly with the fundamental questions arising at every point of his life. He sees his faith applicable to daily issues of bread, job, sex,

evil, pain, and crisis. Doubts may arise at every point but he
faces them courageously. His faith is not gullible or defensive.

EMOTION BY ITSELF CAN MISLEAD

Peter Berger says, "When an individual ceases to grapple
intellectually with the problems posed by his religion, feeling
takes the place of thought. Another substitution of questions
takes place here. The individual no longer asks, What is the
truth? Instead, he asks, What do I feel? And that is but one
step to the next question: How does this make me feel? Emotional pragmatism now takes the place of the honest confrontation with the Christian message." Feeling, by itself, can be
a terribly misleading guide. One is tempted also to ask what
others feel or think, as a primary base for belief. Emotion
alone is inadequate.

Have you ever had the experience of listening to a spell-
binding speaker who was able to pull you into his sphere of
thinking by the sheer magnetism of face, gesture, and emotion? Past generations have known such persons in the realm
of politics and religion. Our day has such demagogues also.
Some are religious leaders, some are politicians. Some are a
strange mixture of the two. To allow emotion without intelligent faith to dominate your response is to be left vulnerable
to their half-truths and blatant errors.

FAITH AND REASON ARE FRIENDS

By all means, allow faith and reason to be allies. In Christian experience they are not mutually exclusive. Faith involves not only firm commitment to true reality, but also firm
conviction that reality is there awaiting your clearer understanding. Faith is not belief without basis. It *is* saving power,
bringing enlightenment, courage, and capacity to overcome
temptation.

In an age of instant tea and instant soup, avoid the temptation to seek instant answers and instant eternal truth. In a search for truth which ignores its built-in subtlety and the complexity of the human situation to which it speaks, one may seek only the obvious that can be extracted in half-serious haste. But truth cannot be packaged. It will not submit to momentary formulas.

Each tends to see and understand through his own personality filter. Ruth Benedict has pointed this out: "No man ever looks at the world with pristine eyes. He sees it edited by a definite set of customs and institutions and ways of thinking. Even in his philosophical probings he cannot go behind these stereotypes. . . . From the moment of his birth the customs into which he is born shape his experience and behavior. By the time he can talk, he is the little creature of his culture, and by the time he is grown and able to take part in its activities, its habits are his habits, its beliefs his beliefs, its impossibilities his impossibilities." When you demand immediately to see all, hear all, and know all you are letting yourself in for premature and obviously inadequate conclusions.

TRUTH SEEKING MAKES US GROW UP

Your search for truth, including your honest confrontation with doubt, can be a means toward spiritual maturity. If you genuinely seek authenticity, then you are going to be conscious of personal growth. You will yourself burst your "I have arrived" bubble. This false sense of achievement is sometimes motivated by pride. Alfred North Whitehead liked to say, "Not ignorance, but the ignorance of ignorance is the death of knowledge." Complacency can also motivate in you a false sense of achievement. It may be wise to be content with what you have at the moment, but it is never wise to be content with what you are. An automatic pilot may work for a time in an airplane but there is no automatic pilot for your brain and your spirit. Complacency is sometimes born out of a cocky satisfaction with an earlier faith experience. When one gives testimony of his faith, he may be prone to share only the first remembrance of his encounter with Christ. It is as though nothing else has ever happened since. He has been drifting since his first assertion, "I believe!"

YOU HAVEN'T ARRIVED

But there is ample proof that you haven't yet "arrived." For one thing, your knowledge is limited. Man's brain has twelve billion or more cells, yet research concludes that the average one of us uses only 10 per cent of his mind. At our best our mind is still limited. Even the fantastic machines we have built with our brilliance cannot give total knowledge or answer all questions. The most learned astronomer touches only the fringe of the immensity of the universe. The mathematical genius is limited by time and by his capacity to make errors which throw him off course. The theologian and the philosopher think and develop their systems through finiteness. The physician, constantly conquering new disease, is still outwitted by heart disease and cancer, the two major man killers. Indeed, we know in part. This makes the search for truth all the more exciting.

Proof that we have not yet arrived is also seen in the incompleteness of our character. Robotlike human perfection is neither possible nor desirable. Even the finest of men have moral chinks in their armor. Our age as the ages before us is plagued by hate, war, violence, slander, and hypocrisy. The ideal of Christ, the man for others, is still but an ideal. We have not arrived. We confess, "Not that I have already obtained this or am perfect; but I press on to make it my own, because Christ Jesus has made me his own" (Phil. 3:12 RSV).

You have not arrived, and you and the rest of us know it. Here then is truth: You are still on the way. Excitement can accompany you in the discovery of what that way may bring. You are man, a decision-making creature blessed with the freedom to choose among a variety of possibilities. Let truth be the key to your final choices. Down through the ages Christians have recorded guidelines to truth which are available to you as tangible reference points today. These are included in the Bible, in the prayers and history of the church, in books on theology and ethics, in the pronouncements and resolutions of national and world church bodies, and in the personal counsel of lay and clerical leaders.

TRUTH BECOMES A WAY OF LIFE

Out of this whole background come certain truths regarding God and man which form a frame of reference for you as you confront your contemporary world. If these truths seem to remain cold and lifeless to you, without resulting in Christian action, it may be because they have not become a part of your life. Internalization must take place. Truth becomes a way of life for you rather than mere intellectual points of reference outside yourself. This internalization is what we have already referred to as the wedding of belief and commitment. You trust your life to God and his service.

This trustful commitment to truth must be realistic. This is both its pain and its excitement. The truth of God's love as seen in Christ must not gloss over the cruel facts of our world. The cross is at the center of human history. The truth we commit ourselves to is not simply that God is love, but rather that God revealed his love in Jesus Christ, terribly crucified. This revelation does not calm our fears nor does it lead us away from its terrible moment. Instead we are led into the very midst of the worst of human nature and of man's vilest passions. There we are met by God. The calling is to live the same life of faith and love which led Christ to that awesome cross. Truth is a strong dose on those terms.

Little wonder then that we are afraid. Sweat breaks out. A hard lump rises in the throat and in the belly when we become aware of what God expects of us both in belief and in action. At the same time truth will definitely find a way to break the conspiracy of silence and make of us its mouthpiece. Truth still triumphs.

The classic moment in a bullfight occurs when the bullfighter faces his wounded adversary prior to attempting to wield the death blow behind the head. The Spanish call it "the moment of truth." Such a moment of truth is being experienced in many ways on the current scene. The early days of the nonviolent movement among American Negroes brought a moment of truth to many cities. Prejudice saw its brutal face in the mirror for the first time. The strain of violence just beneath the surface of respectability was exposed. The truth of freedom became a rallying cry. For whenever one man begins to understand the truth under God that he is made in God's image, he can never be a slave again. This is true in the realm of race. This is also true in the realm of religious belief. This is true wherever man finds himself a bond slave of whatever system, practice, lie, or tyranny.

Chapter

3

Discovering the
Real You: Repentance

THE WORLD, troubled though it is, is a fascinating stage. The drama of discipleship is exciting. The truth about your world and your place in it is a never-ending discovery. Before you find your role, however, you must find yourself. The question of life's purpose is rooted in identity. "What shall I do?" is involved with "Who am I?"

"WHO AM I?"

The struggle with the question "Who am I?" is at the very heart of your life. From every angle, there are attempts to help you find the answers. Psychology, sociology, psychiatry, and religion all converge to give clues and answers. The question is far more than a lifelong riddle, however.

The question is made problematic by our frequent attempts to be someone or something else. The great American pastime is to idolize certain figures and adopt the trademark features of those persons as one's own. In past days the pacesetters were such personalities as Rudolph Valentino, Jean

Harlow, Charles Lindbergh, and Franklin D. Roosevelt. Their personality features, and sometimes even their voices, were copied by men and women in many places. In the religious realm, from pulpits, you could hear the copied voices and words of George Truett, Harry Emerson Fosdick, or Billy Sunday.

More recently, the lionized and copied have been the Beatles and Brigitte Bardot or, in another realm, John F. Kennedy and Martin Luther King. People tend to follow trends, patterns, and fads. Sometimes genuine hero worship is involved. At other times, however, self-identity is so painful that it is easier to follow the crowd's worship of a personality.

What do you say about yourself? Let us say you become involved in a bit of drinking one night at a party. You say and do some things out of character for you. The next day you look in the mirror and say, "But I wasn't myself!"

Or perhaps in an argument with a friend, you suddenly find yourself on the losing end and begin to "blow your stack." You express yourself in extremes. You may receive some enjoyment at the moment in being able thus to ventilate. But later you say to yourself, "I hate myself when I do that!"

Or perhaps you are caught in a time of crisis and the alternatives are all difficult and costly. You lack judgment and counsel and feel yourself on the brink of near-disaster. Looking back, from a more objective viewpoint, you say to yourself, "I was almost out of my mind."

Or you have an assignment, perhaps a public speech, and find yourself literally tied in knots. You keep an undercurrent of conversation going with yourself: "Let yourself go . . . stay loose . . . just be natural . . . be yourself."

All these situations illustrate the fact that often we find

ourselves at war within ourselves. There are life situations which begin to peel away the exterior to show the real person. The importance of the self, one's true identity, is highlighted in times of stress or decision. When an individual is dominated mainly by minor drives, by compulsions, or by chance winds of circumstance, he loses his integrity. Major directions of purpose grow out of the knowledge of the real you. Long-range goals indicate maturity and health. For some people only the expectancy of immediate pleasure has any importance. Such shortsighted living is mandatory when people do not know who they are.

Life-style involves not only how you live each segment of life but the overriding purpose which catches up each unit into the whole. The healthiest and best fulfilled persons are those who are able to live the minutes and the days with meaning because they have a sense of who they are and what they are about.

THE MASK

The fragmented life results from many things. For one, we tend to wear a mask of sorts to cover our real person. Sometimes we do this because we do not know who we are. Sometimes we do it because we are afraid of who we are. Sometimes the mask is assumed to hide who we are. Masks can be convenient, but they can also be dangerous. They can even be ludicrous.

A touring group of French mime artists pointed up what masks can do. The group wore masks portraying hilarity in their first scene. The eyes were alive, the mouth was turned up in a broad and leering grin. The bodies of the actors responded to the personality of the mask. They exhibited excitement, happiness, and abandonment in their actions. At one point the actors removed their masks to reveal yet another mask in which the facial characteristics were the opposite. The mouth turned down in a broad and heavy scowl. The eyes were narrowed and the lines of the forehead drawn tight. Immediately their bodies began to droop and to sag. The shoulders slumped and the legs seemed heavy.

There was one exception. One of the actors had not removed his mask and even though his body was carrying out the movement of sadness and depression, fixed to his face was the mask of hilarity. He tugged frantically, but it would not budge. The audience empathized and was made uncomfortable. The truth the actors desired hit home. One's face and one's body are but symbols of the need for wholeness and harmony between body and spirit. This is what is involved in finding yourself in God and living by what you find·

WHAT IS MAN?

A Natural Being?

Philosophers have attempted to approach man by various views or categories. One school says that man is a natural being, a highly complex place where influences and forces meet to play upon him. These tend to mold, change, or stimulate him. Marxist communism and fascism tend to follow such a view. The way we treat one another or even look upon ourselves is important. If man is little more than a human being who is to be manipulated or played upon as an instrument, then what hope is there to establish unique personal identity through Jesus?

A Shrine of Truth and Beauty?

Another philosophical view is the cultural one which says that human life by means of science, technology, and culture can be made a shrine of truth and beauty. This view is beautiful, but ignores the fact of the brutality of life and the willfulness of man.

A Creature of the Here-and-Now?

Yet another view regards life to be lived here and now, fully, with no holds or limits. Energy and dynamism make such a view attractive. Leaders, inspired, instinctive, and passionate, grow out of such a self-concept. At the same time, the great host of people do not have the basic stuff of life to understand this as a possibility.

A Digit?

Yet another view would place man in a collectivist society. The meaning of life for him would be comprehended only in terms of the social group to which he belongs, or in which he is imprisoned. The determinism of this view and the thought of man's being utterly lost in the crowd make it a morbid one.

Undoubtedly all these views have elements of truth and all together have left their mark on man and his search to know himself. No one of them, however, is adequate for describing man and his life situation. He is more than all these. His problems and his potential are more than these.

WHAT IS MAN'S PURPOSE?

At all levels—food, work, sex, human relations—man presses toward a purpose which may be either positive or negative. He finally confronts an ultimate situation at each of these levels which presents questions for which he must have an answer. In all these questions and human situations, man is shapeless, undefined, and confused until he is confronted with some way of salvation. Until all the parts of his life begin to fit together with some kind of meaning, he is not a full man.

We are all plagued by false purposes and by false selves. In myriad ways every day, the true self is challenged. We have inklings that we would not really be satisfied with riches and power if we had them. We suspect that while today may

be a gay one, tomorrow will be dull. We sense that our selfishness will only satisfy us for an hour or so and that crushing
someone else by pride or prejudice is not our highest self. We
get an idea of what Paul meant when he talked about "putting off the old self and putting on the new." "Putting on
Christ" is the self identifying with the highest possibility
available for life.

WHY REPENT?

Repentance is integral to the search for self. So much
camouflage, rebellion, sin, hopelessness, and confusion have
distorted the self that repentance is necessary. As Paul Tillich said (in *The Shaking of the Foundations*), "Man is split
within himself. Life moves against itself through aggression,
hate, and despair. We are wont to condemn self-love, but
what we really mean to condemn is contrary to self-love. It is
that mixture of selfishness and self-hate that permanently
pursues us, that prevents us from loving others, and that pro-
hibits us from losing ourselves in the love with which we are
loved eternally. He who is able to love himself is able to love
others also; he who has learned to overcome self-contempt
has overcome his contempt for others. But the depth of our
separation lies in just the fact that we are not capable of a
great and merciful divine love toward ourselves. On the contrary, in each of us there is an instinct of self-destruction,
which is as strong as our instinct of self-preservation. . . .
Without the help of modern psychology, Paul expressed the
fact in his famous words, 'For I do not do the good I desire,
but rather the evil that I do not desire.' " The Apostle Paul
was estranged even from himself and recognized the fact as
sin.

THE PRODIGAL: A PARABLE OF REPENTANCE

A clear insight into the need for repentance is seen in the
parable of the prodigal. Two figures in the parable give us

insight into our search for the real self. Both the elder brother and the younger had their problems. In reality, every man is pictured in the parable. You know the story well. In contemporary language it might sound even more familiar.

A youth left his home in the city to try his wings in a new place and at a new job. Eager to taste every exciting experience possible, he became indiscriminate in his choice of friends and activities. He conformed to his environment and lost his old moral values. His job suffered and was finally lost. His landlord locked his room and held his possessions for failure to pay his rent. His companions who had been mooching off him began to drift away since he could no longer keep up his heady style of living. Hungry and friendless, he was too ashamed to tell his family. Weeks drifted by.

Finally when he found himself tempted to escape his plight through drugs, he knew he had reached the bottom. He hitchhiked home and presented himself to his father as a miserable failure. He cast himself on him for his forgiveness. In his despair he had realized that his father had not stopped loving him even though he was dirty and a failure and had spent all his money. Love on both sides had made it possible for him to ask for and receive forgiveness.

Hovering in the background, however, is an almost unnoticed second figure. An older brother, who had stayed at home, kept his job, and lived a relatively moral life, was deeply resentful. Jealous of the younger brother's reception, he felt the young profligate should be ostracized. He felt his brother was inferior in contrast to himself and his own habits of hard work and uprightness. His jealousy and anger consumed him so that he refused to have a part in the loving and grateful reception given for the younger brother.

In this contemporary nutshell is a picture of the kind of unrepentant qualities which keep men from becoming whole. For the prodigal, the story is one of irresponsibility. Without concern for family, friends, or future, he nearly destroys himself in self-centered living. He wastes time, money, and precious energy. He is torn and divided because he is living against everything which he knows to be right and meaningful. Thinking he is dedicated to the pursuit of free will, he becomes instead enslaved to habits and patterns of life which are destructive. The power of his own will is not great enough to overcome these habits. He is estranged from family, home and life itself. Ultimately he sees his alienation from himself. He becomes disgusted with himself and the futility of his existence.

This prodigal youth discovers that he gets in deeper and deeper with every act of rebellion or wastefulness of life. His predicament centers in the fact that his problems are insoluble with the resources he has. There seems no way out. He begins to face up to the fact of the grandeur and misery which have been at war within him. He longs for the grandeur but finds life always issuing only in the misery.

He is mortal. But he has pretended to be above the consequences of his immorality. Therein is his great sin! He has pretended to be that which he is not and cannot be. What began as a free-wheeling, uninhibited pattern of life has bogged down in enslavement to bread, lust, and momentary pleasure. He tries to carry out incompatible purposes: fulfillment and mere self-gratification. Consequently he is unable to achieve any purpose at all.

He is one-sided and disoriented. His life is out of focus. He contradicts the meaning of his life by seeking to commit himself only to that which will give him pleasure.

His real problem is not to be found just in the sins and acts which characterize him. His problem is his total state of mind and heart, out of which all these acts issue as sick fruit from a sick tree. That which he thought was going to be glossy and appealing becomes ugly and distasteful. A whole chain of circumstances has been set in motion by his first wrong choices and his inability to be honest about what is happening to him.

Wrong tends to give birth to wrong, and starts a chain of accident and disharmony which quickly develop a will of their own. The resulting circumstances exact their own toll and run their course to the bitter end, before an individual is able to break free of them again.

It is in such patterns that alcoholics and narcotic addicts are trapped. The compulsive gambler finds himself caught in a web of circumstances which rush him on to results he could never have purposed. Like a stone thrown in water, the widening circle of wrong acts reaches far beyond one person. Wrong being and wrong behavior are never just private transactions of one man. Rarely is sin against God alone. Bigotry, graft, corruption of justice, mob spirit, militarism, class contempt, and individual acts of immorality all affect a wide spectrum of persons. Many persons are involved in our wasteful and unrepentent living.

The alibi habit is easily developed also. Obviously the prodigal youth often rationalized his behavior by calling it freedom, or colorful or exciting action. To be honest with oneself about oneself is impossible without repentance.

Do not overlook the other figure in the story. The older brother is a key to understanding self also. His basic patterns of work and personal morality may have been excellent. But his human relations were poor. He was right-doing but loveless. Man probably never sins more deeply than when he thinks he is being and doing good. Pride is usually the basis of the lack of mercy. To judge oneself on the basis of contrast with other's errors and frailities is to be blind. The older brother may not have been guilty of the sins of the flesh but the sins of the spirit were his. Jealousy, anger, greed, and fear all probably were in his makeup. He was jealous of a brother who could inspire love in spite of his sinfulness. He was angry that he himself was not exalted because of his own hard work. Yet his hard work may only have been motivated by greed. At any rate, he resented the family's means being used to throw a banquet for his returning brother. He had no sense of loving and grateful abandonment because of the returned one who had been supposed lost. He feared competition, perhaps, with this attractive sinner. His own staleness and triteness were possibly obnoxious to himself.

Jesus often pointed out the cruelty of righteous people and he opposed self-righteousness on the part of the right-doing. Some of the most religiously active people are also extremely hateful. The radical preference of God is for love above mere. right-doing. Time and again Jesus turned to otherwise disreputable people to show his love and to be willing to receive theirs. Self-righteous men around him condemned him. Their own lovelessness and rejection of others was heightened by their unwillingness to understand his love.

Thus these contrasting pictures of the prodigal and the older brother point up much of human nature. Look at them both. You will find something of yourself there if you have eyes to see, ears to hear, and the willingness to understand what you see and hear. This may be a place of self-discovery for you. Christian faith at its best provides a climate for confession and repentance to take place. For the "elder son" type of person a shattering of his self-centered self is involved. Insight into his own pride and unconcern for the personhood of others is necessary.

For the "prodigal type," his moment of truth comes in the honest confession of his own inadequacy. He becomes willing to believe in God's willingness to help him bear his insurmountable problems. He believes God yearns for him to be stronger. He recognizes that God will not hold his past against him. He confesses, "I can will what is right but I cannot do it."

WHAT IS REPENTANCE?

Repentance then involves facing self honestly and with recognition of need. More than sorrow for the past and chagrin over the present occurs in repentance, although contrition is obviously present. A new mood, attitude, and disposition toward life take place. Repentance then is a turning or conversion in which one submits to the lordship of Jesus Christ. It is a radical turning from the way of self-love, self-assertion, and self-trust to the way of obedient trust and commitment to God and his world. This recognition of a higher source and meaning for life takes away from one the need to make of himself a God-like creature. Recognition of God's wisdom and care for the human person is an insight which can produce humility, moral realism, and readiness for commitment to the adventure of life.

It is exceedingly difficult in this success-oriented world to confess we are wrong and in repentance to seek to do right. The difficulty is experienced time and again in human relationships. A young and rather green missionary discovered how difficult pride and stubbornness can be. In conversation with an experienced Latin American pastor, he determined that a certain program was going to be done exactly the way it had been done in the United States. Because of the success of the project in its North American context, the missionary exerted high pressure to force the use of the same program in his adopted country of ministry. The Latin pastor insisted that failure would result because of the inappropriateness of the program to the culture. The missionary prevailed. The project was a disastrous failure. Confused, aware of his humanity, and embarrassed by his stubbornness, the missionary became deeply repentant. He went to the Latin American pastor to confess his error and to ask forgiveness. The pastor replied in unforgettable words, "We shall always have an open door between us now, for you have come to me today as a man rather than as God."

When confession and repentance build bridges between men, how significant is the experience to their personal discovery of God and of self. Without morbidness or self-deception, confession admits guilt and inadequacy. Excuses and alibis are stripped away. The causes and consequences of wrongdoing can be faced squarely.

UNREPENTANT MAN

Without repentance, man is so much his own God that he cannot sense his need to know the true God. Unrepentant man is a problem to himself, whether his nature be that of the prodigal or of the older brother. Alienation, contradictoriness, and feebleness of human existence are his characteristics. He is defensive. He sets up his own little kingdom, puts himself on the throne, dogmatically ascribes his code of beliefs, makes himself his own moral police force, and does it all in the name of the God he denies by perpetrating this. The unrepentant person is blocked from establishing his true identity. Charles Boddie has contributed a bit of poetic fantasy which applies to the unrepentant:

> What a queer bird the frog are.
> When he sit he stand, almost.
> When he walk he fly, almost.
> When he sing he cry, almost.
> He ain't got no sense, hardly.
> He ain't got no tail, hardly, either.
> He sit on what he ain't got, almost.

Everything you say about an unrepentant man has to be countered with the word "almost." He never really comes into his own.

Confession, repentance, and forgiveness are basic to the discovery of the real you. Confession is the beginning place in the voluntary stripping away of the mask one wears. It is a stated awareness that "that which I would, I do not." It is a personal admission of moral guilt. Such a confession from one's inner being is not easy. You tend to look for scapegoats or for oversimplified rationalizations rather than simply to say with candor, "Forgive me." The scriptural portrayal of Jesus which states that "he emptied himself" is a guideline for our own lives. Until self-emptying is a part of your Christian experience you have not truly begun to understand discipleship.

WHAT HAPPENS WHEN YOU REPENT?

In repentance you do not argue with God about your place in history but simply state your willingness to participate in history with grace and courage. Repentance cuts through the lesser questions. Rather than ask trifles such as "What will people think?" "Will I look silly?" "Can I get by?" one becomes involved with the larger questions of "What is true, good, and just?" The entire restructuring of life occurs. Insensitivity and pride give way to compassion and sensitivity. Your goals and ambitions are poured through repentance and forgiveness into a new mold for life. You can never be the same man again. Many new ethical demands will begin to challenge your life because of God's forgiveness.

THE EXPERIENCE OF FORGIVENESS

Discovery of the real self, of God's creation, is bound up then with repentance and forgiveness. Repentance becomes the trustful acceptance of the full truth about ourselves and others rather than evasion of that truth. We are thus made whole through being enabled to bring ourselves with our possibilities and limitations into the open, knowing that we shall not be rejected. We are not saved through trying to obliterate ourselves and our difficulties. We do not have to live through a substitute life of sorts. Camouflage is no longer necessary. The disruptive tension between our actual and our desired selves is broken. Rather than having to deal with ourselves in fantasy, excuses, or cynicism, we are able to cope realistically. No portrait artist is needed to falsify the picture of our lives, nor to accentuate the few positives, nor to shade out the negatives. We may be portrayed in clear, bold strokes because we have realistically confessed our need. We have experienced God's forgiveness.

Few experiences mean more. No matter how estranged from life a person has been, forgiveness breaks through to him. In turn, the one who has experienced forgiveness is enabled to accept others previously unacceptable. Forgiveness is unconditional. We cannot earn it. At the same time we cannot love unless we have accepted forgiveness. The greater the experience of forgiveness, usually the greater the love. Many times in New Testament encounters between Jesus and other persons one reads of the experience of forgiveness. A prostitute rejected by everyone else finds herself pouring out her grateful love to Jesus who had insight into her need and accepted her. So it is with criminals who have been forgiven for their crimes by the victims of their criminal acts and thus experience overwhelming change of mind and purpose of life. A new perspective for life results.

Paul Tillich said in *The New Being:* "And he who loves is also able to accept life and to love it. This is not the same as to love God. For many pious people in all generations the love of God is the other side of the hatred for life. And there is much hostility towards life in all of us, even in those who have completely surrendered to life. Our hostility towards life is manifested in cynicism and disgust, in bitterness and continuous accusation against life. We feel rejected by life, not so much because of its objective darkness and threats and horrors, but because of our estrangement from its power and meaning. He who is reunited with God, the creative Ground of life, the power of life in everything that lives, is reunited with life. He feels accepted by it and he can love it. He understands that the greater love is, the greater the estrangement which is conquered by it. In metaphorical language I should like to say to those who feel deeply their hostility towards life: Life accepts you; life loves you as a separated part of itself; life wants to reunite you with itself, even when it seems to destroy you." To be forgiven is to be accepted and to be accepted is to be given the power to integrate one's life and to find purpose.

To experience forgiveness is not conditioned upon first being perfect, but upon confessing need and recognizing the source of help. Change is not the condition but the result of forgiveness. It is not mere godly indulgence, nor token tolerance of human foibles. Rather, a change, a dynamic new being, is involved. A transition from a state of guilt, conflict, and helplessness occurs to bring release from guilt, leading to achieved wholeness, strength, and happiness. The whole experience of repentance and forgiveness is more than just one ecstatic moment in life. A continuous and lifelong process is involved. Once set in motion, forgiveness is a continuing bridge builder between man and God and between man and man. The power of forgiveness to transform all life and relationships is incredible. "Love as forgiveness is the most difficult and impossible of moral achievements. Yet it is a possibility if the impossibility of love is recognized and the sin in the self is acknowledged. Therefore an ethic culminating in impossible possibility produces its choicest fruit in terms of the doctrine of forgiveness, the demand that the evil in the other shall be borne without vindictiveness because the evil in the self is known." Reinhold Niebuhr has here captured the subtle power of forgiveness in recognizing its leveling and humanizing influence in relationships between men.

Neither guilt nor tyrannical conscience can continue to make a man captive if he has experienced repentance and forgiveness. While guilt may be a sign that we are not totally insensitive to wrongdoing, it becomes sick guilt when it is unabated and unresolved. On the other hand, when guilt is gone, neither apathy nor conceit continue to hold sway. Love born of forgiveness is free from the distortions that result from seeking one's own advantage always over others and from attaching undue importance to one's own concerns. One's possessions, ambitions, family, and nation all fall into a healthy and balanced pattern rather than being the ultimates for which one fights animallike. True, forgiveness does not destroy selfishness, but one who has insight into the evil within himself is far different from one who simply accepts human egoism as a force which must somehow be balanced with charity in order to be moral.

Repentance and forgiveness bring the healthful knowledge that you are not alone. A young couple went through the terrible experience of the rapid illness and death of their beloved five-year-old child. Leukemia claimed as victim this bright life and joyful spirit. While the mother and father might have sunk into the oblivion of self-pity and mourning, they were enabled to say through their sorrow, "We can bear it not so much because we know God, but because he knows us."

What a difference this knowledge of the acceptance of God in Christ can make to the meaning and significance of life. To recognize the love of God poured out in the person of Jesus Christ in the crucifixion is to gain new insight into one's self. It is not so much that you are tempted to say that the cross he is dying on is really *your* cross. Rather you may feel, "I am dying there." You recognize that the suffering of Jesus was not to keep you from suffering but because you were already suffering and your suffering seemed senseless. He knows you. In turning your life to him you are free to be the one he means you to be.

God:

Take fire and burn away our guilt and our lying hypocrisies.

Take water and wash away our brother's blood which we have caused to be shed.

Take hot sunlight and dry the tears of those we have hurt, and heal their wounded souls, minds, and bodies.

Take love and root it in our hearts, so that brotherhood may grow, transforming the dry desert of our prejudices and hatreds.

Take our imperfect prayers and purify them so that we mean what we pray and are prepared to give ourselves to you along with our words, through Jesus Christ, who did not disdain to take our humanness upon him and live among us, sharing our life, our joys, and our pains.

Amen.

—From Malcolm Boyd,
Are You Running With Me Jesus?

Chapter

4

Better Than Whistling
in the Dark: Courage

The search for contemporary men of courage is unfortunately seldom pursued among today's churches. Too often churchmen have been merely proper, stuffy, and cautious. Generally courage is sought among adventurers, soldiers, and a few statesmen. Or, we automatically look back through the centuries to Homer, Alexander the Great, Richard the Lion Hearted, Columbus, or Daniel Boone. Novels, movies, and daydreams transport us to other ages and to other men's battles for a look at courage.

A group of students at coffee break on a state college campus tossed around the idea of what life must have been like in pioneer days in the United States. Incredibly, one student said he really wished he could have lived then when men had something to live and fight for. His reveries conjured up visions of man pitted against nature, man conquering virgin territory, and man protecting his loved ones from Indians and wild animals. Like many others today, the student was mistakenly harkening back to another man's battles and another age's problems. He may have been wistfully looking back because those battles have already been fought, and won or lost. His own battles are before him and his need for courage sticks in his throat.

THE CHRISTIAN: A COURAGEOUS GADFLY

Courage is a live alternative for today's Christian. The current scene is a boot camp for discipleship. To be a follower of Christ is to be drawn each day down new roads and into dramatic events demanding courage. Today's youth are the shock troops engaged in the painful process of breaking old customs and political structures which will not meet today's needs. This new impatient and critical crop of young gadflies is fearful only of the complacent and the passive.

When people are young, they are expected to make major attacks upon the established order with intent to reform it. The individual who courageously gets involved may find a chance to define himself and to discover his own values. A high school or college student ought to refuse to be a citizen in exile. He is not absolved of responsibility to society. He ought not to tolerate the denial of rights and responsibilities. His vigorous mind and body can be channeled to tasks which will bring hope and new life to his community and his world. Students in our country have been involved in the action and policy arenas on major social issues. Many have had tremendous organizational effectiveness. This effectiveness has been applied with courage to the situations of human rights, poverty, illiteracy, and concern for peace.

MORE THAN NONCONFORMITY

At the same time there is a decided difference between courage and mere nonconformity. Nonconformity for the sake of nonconformity can be gross in its results. The nonconformist may be only intellectually arrogant or socially irresponsible. He may have an exaggerated self-esteem and be dominated by selfishness. The nonconformist sometimes only wallows in self-pity, undisciplined talent, and a pre-occupation with self-gratification. It is true that nonconform-ist behavior in dress or habits can be terribly irritating to adults. The rebelliousness of the nonconformist per se should not, however, be equated with courage.

COURAGE GOES WITH RESPONSIBILITY

Courage comes with a sense of responsibility. Indeed there may be some irreverance on the part of the youth who dares to say "I don't give a damn" about the self-interests of some communities and institutions. Such irreverence, but tem-pered by love and responsibility, is to be sought for. The individual who has moral courage confronts the resulting opposition and hostility without panicking or retreating.

For example, in relationships to government, dissent and disloyalty should not be equated. To be both critic and friend of government is the happy but delicate balance a genuine Christian citizen seeks. When government or community or church seeks to silence criticism and to intimidate critics, democratic procedures are violated. A good example from history is the issue of slavery. At one time in certain areas of our nation, teachers who attacked slavery were deprived of their posts. Editors who dared to call for abolition lost their papers. Clergymen who raised the moral issues of human rights were forced out of their pulpits. Books were burned. In the end, the critics were silenced and parts of the South closed ranks against the critics, and thus closed their minds. Today's racial struggle is part of the product of that time of intimidation.

THE STUFF OF AN EXCITING LIFE

Courage is a vital part of contemporary Christian disciple-ship. The people who consistently meet the ethical demands upon their lives with courage do not have to "whistle in the dark." The task may be difficult but the way seems clear. The dull tedium of life without courage is a terrible prospect. Someone has said that such a life seems much like getting a daily mailbag full of second class matter. There are no pinnacles. There are no challenges. There are no dilemmas to be faced honestly. There is no rise of the blood to the head, no surge of adrenalin in the veins. The heart is not quickened, nor the mind sharpened. On the other hand, when one is committed to courageous living, he tingles to his fingertips with a sense of urgency. For him life is worth living. And it is worth living on today's terms. He fights today's battles rather than merely dreams of yesterday's. Courage provides new perspective for his life. Courage is a fuel for living that gives extra mileage.

You, like most, have probably been well-meaning in your desire to live vigorously and courageously. You dream great dreams of conquest. You imagine how well you shall perform in the hour of crisis. Idealism overflows when you think of a challenging vocation. The mind plays longingly with a willingness to go anywhere and to do anything.

The realistic end of such well-meaning dreaming is seen in Robert Anderson's sophisticated lines: "His *Walden* now the *Wall Street Journal,* His jug of wine a double-scotch, O, addled Adonais! He dreamed his life in poetry, but lives it out in prose, Not lonely on a peak in Darien, but jammed into the Greenwich local home; on Saturdays smiling, he pushes carts through supermarts, Homosapiens homogenized!" Many a revolutionary spirit of yesterday is a domesticated conservative today. Social activist collegians often turn into cautious and stuffy alumni. The poetic idealist can sadly become a moneygrubber. The sensitive spirit is too easily crusted over by harsh treatment. As my colleague,

Ross Coggins, often says, "The bland lead the bland." Only two kinds of endeavor appear obvious: the cautious and the super-cautious. The "non-boat-rockers" predominate.

Reuel Howe's words are instructive: "How can the drag-ging tug of a reactionary spirit be overcome and men find in their faith the courage to be and do? A spirit of timidity clutches at us constantly and threatens to choke our crea-tivity, especially when life challenges us by crises growing out of all the 'changes and chances of this mortal life.' Many examples are to be found in both ancient and modern life.

"Moses in response to God's call to deliver the Jews out of Egypt, reflected the spirit of timidity when he said in his conversation with the Spirit of God, 'Who am I that I should go?' or again, 'They will not believe me or listen to my voice'; or still again, 'O Lord, I am not eloquent but slow of tongue and speech.' Likewise, when Jeremiah the Prophet was called, he pleaded, 'Ah Lord, behold I do not know how to speak for I am only a youth.'

"In times of crisis people tend to withdraw timidly. . . . The spirit of timidity is afraid of life, afraid of facing its problems. It causes men to use their institutions and forms as places in which to hide from the challenges of new life and truth, and to evade or compromise the great human issues."

COURAGE GIVES PERSPECTIVE

Courage from God helps us see how idle our promises and our dreams can be. Such courage indeed gives us perspective on who we are and what we are doing. Courage like this can be a mirror held up to show us how we really look. We are brave as long as we are far from battle. We can make strong statements as long as we are surrounded by friends who con-firm what we believe. We can criticize the establishment as long as we think we are too young to do anything about it.

Or if we are part of the power structure we can always say that someone higher up is to blame. The Nürnberg war crimes trials demonstrated this repeatedly. Germans on trial for involvement in Hitler-age atrocities blamed the Nazi structure and passed the buck up the line to a ranking officer or politico. Courage dies in buck-passing!

Dante reserved the hottest places in hell for those who in time of moral and political crisis attempted to maintain their neutrality. He obviously would have something to say (and it would not be too discreet) to those today who are saying, "You can't mix religion and politics"; "You can't legislate morality"; "My business will be ruined"; "We will lose some of the best givers in the church"; "Property values will go down"; "Let the church stick to preaching the gospel!"; "God's on our side!"

Yet in the midst of these disclaimers and the inaction they represent, a minority of churchmen have assumed heroic size. And . . . a group of young Americans, some through Christian motivation, have discovered the new vocation of politically activating the politically inert and the politically excluded. And . . . a few churches of various denominations have experienced the birth pains of spiritual renewal through involvement in the ills of man.

FRONTIERS FOR COURAGE

But there is too little such excitement. Much of our energy is spent in celebrating our shifts from anti-Christian to sub-Christian points of view. In spite of the achievements in the realm of civil rights, economic opportunity, and social concern, we are ill at ease because deep in our bones we know that these apparent advances are merely righting the accumulated neglect of generations. Yet some are guilty of saying: "Civil rights legislation is a fact. OK, Negro Americans, shape up." And hands are washed of responsibility. Can we recognize the vast unfinished tasks still before us?

In our nation's civil rights' struggle, for example, traditional concepts and easygoing communities have been turned upside down. James Baldwin aptly wrote, ". . . the black man has functioned in the white man's world as a fixed star, as an immovable pillar; and as he moves out of his place, heaven and earth are shaken to their foundations." These shaking foundations have tested the mettle of most of the nation's citizens. On both sides of the racial barrier persons have been called to courage. The courage of convictions and the courage of participation have tested the reality of one's faith and commitment. Among the Negroes the stakes have been high: unemployment, imprisonment, possibly death. Among whites who have participated because of militant intolerance of injustice, there have also been awesome risks.

What most of us lack is a sense of destiny. Too easily have we twisted the truth about God and ourselves and our fellowman, or failed even to recognize the truth. Our age has been described eloquently as a "hair-sprayed, avaricious, deodorized, fruging, gossiping, computerized, juvenile worshipping, hate-vomiting, martinied, dyspeptic . . . pill-sucking society, too jaded to identify truth. . . ." A harsh critique!

Instead of vision, we are obsessed by fear. Publicly we are afraid of communism; that is our psychopathic disease. Privately we are afraid of involvement; that is our pathetic illness. We are caught by a creeping disease of the spirit. We do not weep with those who weep, nor hunger with those who hunger. Commercial values dominate, and profit still motivates production, communications, and education. Economic determinism has probably been the major force in bringing racial change to the deep South.

In it all, the worth of man is a fragile concept. Consequently, our white, divorce-ridden society clucks over the assertion that the urban Negro family is a wreck. Expense account executives wonder why the poor are so dirty. Supporters of a giant military budget deplore "crime in the streets."

Against such a backdrop, Jeremiah the prophet becomes excitingly relevant for our times. Listen as he says:

"Thus says the Lord: 'Let not the wise man glory in his wisdom, let not the mighty man glory in his might, let not the rich man glory in his riches; but let him who glories glory in this, that he understands and knows me, that I am the Lord who practices kindness, justice, and righteousness in the earth; for in these things I delight, says the Lord' " (Jer. 9:23–24 RSV).

> "Woe to him who builds his house by unrighteousness,
>   and his upper rooms by injustice;
> who makes his neighbor serve him for nothing,
>   and does not give him his wages;
> who says, 'I will build myself a great house
>   with spacious upper rooms,'
> and cuts out windows for it,
>   paneling it with cedar,
>   and painting it with vermilion.
> Do you think you are a king
>   because you compete in cedar?" (Jer. 22:13–15a RSV).

We can paraphrase to read: Do you think you are a great power because you can deliver missiles and burn villages? Do you think you are great men because of your tenured jobs, or your bank accounts, or the strings you can pull? Do you think you are a great society because you produce the most goods of any nation on earth? Do you think absence

of skin color is an automatic passport to superiority? Hear
Jeremiah again:

"Did not your father eat and drink
  and do justice and righteousness?
  Then it was well with him.
He judged the cause of the poor and needy;
  then it was well.
Is not this to know me?
  says the Lord" (Jer. 22:15b–16 RSV).

CAN THE CHURCH BE COURAGEOUS?

It is thus to ask today: How shall a Christian disciple respond to the revolutions of color, opportunity, and power
now sweeping his world both at home and abroad? Harvey
Cox captures a part of the answer when he talks about the
church as God's avant-garde, whose ties to particular political and cultural arrangements are sufficiently tenuous that
the church is always ready to move to the next stage in history. The church is a people who live in tents, not permanent
temples.

Can Christian institutions shift from rigidity to flexibility
of form, structure, presentation of message, missionary and
evangelistic philosophy? Is it a foregone conclusion that the
churches shall be last-ditch stands of racial exclusivism?
Must ultraconservative economics and politics predominate?
Shall we simply bog down in anti-intellectualism as we confront new science, technology, and a Space Age? Must we
be satisfied with compromised morality as we wink at gross-
ness in business and politics? Dare we attempt to justify war
as a holy crusade of a particularly righteous people who have
God on their side?

Or—may we respond to the excitement of being the dynamic community of Christian faith, committed to proclaim-

ing the truth of the sovereignty of God over all systems, all races, all politics, all parties, all nations, all peoples. This *is* good news! Here *is* hope and excitement! Indeed, let Christians become a "truth corps," debunking the myths of racial superiority and inferiority, rebutting the idea that because you have the poor with you always they should be ignored. Let Christians courageously debunk a false patriotism which proclaims God as the American ally and equates the United States with the kingdom of God. Christian statesman Chief S. O. Adebo, Ambassador of Nigeria to the United Nations, correctly calls us to an allegiance which even transcends allegiance to our individual countries, and that is allegiance to mankind under God.

COURAGE IS RADICAL

Your discipleship must point to the radical nature of the gospel, concerned for the whole man. Carved into the charter of the United Nations, obviously a nonreligious institution, is a dynamic biblical concept calling for "the worth and dignity of the human person." Carve that concept into your life! It is urgent that the community of faith raise Christian questions and take Christian action about the dehumanization of man when he is brutalized by hate and prejudice, or by hunger, or by illiteracy, or by political tyranny, or by war. You should not be embarrassed to preach about *"agape"* love, nor to practice it, even where your enemies are involved.

Courage dies also in mediocrity. Tacitus described Tiberius, the Roman Emperor: "He feared the best, was ashamed of the worst, and chose the innocuous middle." Life, especially Christian life, does not have to end here, however. Such should not be the final word on the church nor the followers of Christ. Even though trial, despair, and finally death marked the course of the Apostle Paul, there was a different spirit about him. He was no god, but he invested his life with courage. In the midst of overwhelming odds, he gave himself to the Christian movement, which had at that hour scarcely made a ripple on the world's surface. He suffered beatings, shipwreck, arrests, and the threat of death. Yet he could describe his life as a triumphal following of Christ. His dominant mood seems to have been, "I can do all things in him who strengthens me" (Phil. 4:13 RSV). Like Paul, we do not have to be empty men.

Yet, Paul was not a superman. He lost his temper. He fought at times with his colleagues. He felt the coldness of old age and the loneliness of prison cells. He was dogmatic at times and rambled in his letters most of the time. But courage was his companion.

Such courage makes one aware that God in Christ knows our humanity. Jesus was not a starry-eyed dreamer unaware of man's frailty. Moffatt translates John's word: "He required no evidence from anyone about human nature. Well did he know what was in human nature" (John 2:25). Christ knew men could be petty, for they had criticized him for works of healing on the Sabbath. He knew that they could be terribly cruel. He knew their vindictiveness. He knew the misery and grandeur which are in man. He knows this in us and does not expect us to perform as supermen. Christ knows our capacity for unparalleled evil but also our capacity to be redeemed for great good.

COURAGE IS PRACTICAL

You do not thus have to make demands beyond reality upon your own stock of courage. Your discipleship in Christ is a fruit of faith. You meet the moral demands of life regardless of how demanding because you serve a moral God. Courage helps you to define first things first. It refuses to sacrifice truth to a shallow harmony and meeting of the mind with one of your fellows. This courage born of God gives you the capacity to say "Yes" when most around you are saying "No" and to say "No" when it is required. The right to say "No" is a final fortress of integrity against forces which would buy you or use you. The capacity to say "Yes" is not enough unless one can also say "No." "Yes-men" are universally suspect. In church-clothing they are none the less so.

Courage is on call especially today when free thinking would be intimidated. The blatant charge of heresy is easily bandied about. Much mental development is cramped and reason cowed by the fear of being branded heretic. Criticism and even common condemnation may be the lot of the "heretic," but truth proceeds only from noble and courageous personalities. The great thinkers from Confucius to the Greek philosophers and from the Renaissance to the present have advocated freedom of mind and freedom of discussion. The conversation of men of conviction is required to air all sides of every major issue. Christian discipleship seeks freedom of such airing of views and convictions. Unity may come through diversity of opinion but true unity never comes through shallow conformity.

BEING TRUE TO YOURSELF

It takes vast courage to live according to one's convictions. This is the reason it is always difficult to act differently from everybody else. Consequently, the easy way out is to pose in ways acceptable to the group or to say that which is acceptable to the group. Sometimes mere silence masks dissent and indicates assent. As soon as you obey your sense of conviction and responsibility, you upset the surface conformity. You can easily be accused of not playing the game. You may possibly be ostracized. Every life is a constant struggle to face the problems which arise and the conflicts which are inherent. You are on the road to maturity when you have the courage to be true to yourself and to assume responsibility for your convictions and your dissatisfaction with the status quo.

This is what living really means. It means accepting risks. "Nothing ventured, nothing gained," says the old proverb. You may think you are being cautious if you refuse to accept such risks, when actually you are denying life. The word of Christ is potent: ". . . whosoever will save his life shall lose it . . ." (Mark 8:35 KJV). If you hesitate and keep on retreating rather than facing the need to express your convictions and to act upon them, you simply become more hesitant. Ultimately you do not even know what your convictions are. However, once you obey the urge within you to assume courageous responsibility, hesitation is swept away. Life regains its meaning and significance. Your true person emerges and you are more relaxed because you know you are being true to yourself under God.

GOALPOSTS FOR LIFE

Courage in discipleship helps to mark out the goalposts for life. Life easily bogs down in meaninglessness. A keen thinker asserts that purpose in life is closely aligned with courage. In *Man's Search For Meaning,* Viktor Frankl tells of his imprisonment during World War II under Nazism. In the discovery of the "why" of his life he had the capacity to endure the "how." He writes, "We knew that we had nothing to lose except our so ridiculously naked lives." Like man in every age, courage became the vehicle which bore him through the worst kinds of torment. In this case, it was the courage of purpose.

On another occasion, Frankl wrote, suffering had become

a task on which he did not want to turn his back. He felt that there was no need to be ashamed of tears when tears bear witness that a man has the greatest courage of all, the courage to suffer.

When life has this kind of perspective great trial and great suffering only make one stronger. Nietzsche firmly believed this. The great Danish philosopher Kierkegaard also believed that suffering was a school for life. Authentic Christianity grows this kind of courage.

At the peak of the Negro's struggle in our nation, the pungency of a Dick Gregory is heard saying: "You didn't die a slave for nothing, Momma. You brought us up. You and all these Negro mothers who gave their kids the strength to go on, to take that thimble to the well while whites were taking buckets. Those of us who weren't destroyed got strength, got callouses on our souls." Many books could be written describing the courage of Christian Negroes in the recent years of racial revolution in our country. History may well record that the rebirth of courage at the heart and purpose of the Christian church is to be seen best in the Negro churches of the South. Not even life was too precious to offer for the cause of justice and freedom. Courage from God gives strength in the midst of danger.

Since courage in Christian discipleship is born of faith, it is a way of life. Courage is not just one momentary heroic act. It is more than a flashing star in the otherwise dull sky of one's life. True courage is the habitual concentration of one's attention on necessary tasks. Courage is self-denial even in unnecessary things. When courage is consistent, then a man can stand like a tower when everything is quaking around him. It is not that he is not afraid but only that he acts in spite of his fear. He knows his courage is rooted in the truth he has discovered about God and his world, and the truth he has discovered about himself. He is able to be openly honest and to face life's difficult times with integrity. Paul Tillich said, "The courage to be is the ethical act in which man affirms his own being in spite of those elements of his existence which conflict with his essential self affirmation."

A young Russian poet, Yevgeny Yevtushenko, has exhibited such courage and honesty in spite of attempts to quiet his prophetic words. Christians have something to learn from thoughts such as his:

You're a brave man they tell me.
I'm not.
Courage has never been my quality.
Only I thought it disproportionate so to degrade myself
   as others did.
No foundations trembled. My voice no more than laughed
   at pompous falsity;
I did no more than write, never denounced, I left out
   nothing I had thought about, defended who deserved
   it, put a brand on the untalented, the ersatz writers
   (doing what had anyhow to be done).
And now they press to tell me that I'm brave.
How sharply our children will be ashamed taking at last
   their vengeance for these horrors remembering how in
   so strange a time common integrity could look like
   courage.

The poet speaks the truth. Because common integrity is uncommon, it often appears courageous.

The businessman who works by Christian ethics requires strength of character to resist cheating and cutthroat competition. The student who befriends a victim of race prejudice may be ridiculed and ostracized. The bystander who comes to the aid of a person under attack may be touted as a hero by some, but a fool by others. The political leader who speaks and votes his convictions may face political isolation or defeat. The revolutionary who seeks to overthrow tyranny lives in the shadow of prison or death.

Courage is the response of a Christian to crisis. It is also his response to every day, every man, and every event he meets.

Chapter

5

Love in Action: Justice

The minister had spoken from texts in Isaiah, "Seek justice, relieve the oppressed, judge the fatherless, plead for the widow," and "What mean ye that ye beat my people to pieces, and grind the faces of the poor?" On the front row a church member nodded assent to the minister's words calling for justice. As he left the worship service, he congratulated the minister for his timely message. The minister could not help but wonder, however, at the paradox of a man who could congratulate a sermon on justice, but continue to receive his major income from substandard slum housing. The minister happened to know that the member had collected his usual weekly rents from the tenants of his squalid rows of houses while en route to the worship service.

In the same congregation that morning was a city councilman. He, too, murmured words of gratitude for the message as he left the church. The minister remembered that only a few weeks before, he had been a vociferous opponent when the city council called for investigation of mismanagement of funds in new school construction. It so happened that this councilman's own building firm had been one of the contractors which had built new buildings with cheap materials. After only one year the schools were already crumbling.

Many miles and states away a group of collegians were interviewing a prominent churchman about his keen interest in Africa. The wealthy churchman personally supported a missionary family in one of the African nations. With characteristic pointedness one of the students asked what the man was doing for the Negro people of his own community. Immediately he engaged the students in a highly prejudiced commentary on the inferiority of Negroes and the inconsiderate pushiness of their civil rights actions.

In another city not far from the first a congregation was singing "In Christ there is no East or West." Even as they sang the stanza, "Join hands, then, brothers of the faith, whate'er your race may be: Who serves my Father as a son Is surely kin to me," a group of ushers was barring entrance to a group of Negroes who had come to worship.

JUSTICE IN LIFE

These three all-too-common scenes depict the great dilemma of the times. Christian love, expressed in abstraction, has not issued in specific justice. Love and justice have been divorced. Yet, justice is love in action. Your pilgrimage of discipleship is called to concrete expression of Christian love. The incongruous situation of love expressed in prayer, hymns, and worship, without corresponding concern for man, is intolerable. Amos needs to thunder again:

> "Your sacred festivals? I hate them, scorn them;
> your sacrifices? I will not smell their smoke;
> you offer me your gifts? I will not take them;
> you offer fatted cattle? I will not look at them.
> No more of your hymns for me!
> I will not listen to your lutes.

No, let justice well up like fresh water,
let honesty roll in full tide" (Amos 5:21–24 Moffatt).

The heart of this ancient message is the fact that the service God desires is justice in the life of man, and not the mere service of formal religion. Amos reminds us today that the subject matter of religion is life and not religion. It was Amos who prophetically and graphically condemned the cruelty of Syria, the slave traffic of Philistia, the treaty breaking of Phoenicia, the unforgiving spirit of Edom, the cruel practices in land grabbing by Gilead, the disregard for human dignity by Moab, the distortion of the law by Judah, and a whole catalog of the social sins of Israel.

THE CHURCH AND SOCIAL ISSUES

But what shall we do with these hard sayings? They are objectionable words in the ears of one who demands that the church not become involved in social issues. This is anathema for one who believes that Christian faith has nothing to do with politics or with life in the secular city. But the meaning is clear. The close relationship between love and justice is vital to contemporary discipleship.

The life and teachings of Jesus Christ are implicit. A researching the Scriptures is important for those who have attempted to say that the message of Jesus spoke only to personal piety. Among the Jewish people of Jesus' day there was discrimination and antagonism toward the Samaritans. Jesus therefore chose a parable of man's concern for man and made the hero a Samaritan. There was great hatred for the Romans who had invaded and conquered the land. Against the backdrop of this hate, Jesus chose a Roman of great character and said "Truly, I say unto you, not even in Israel have I found such faith." The Pharisees were proud and bigoted and Jesus consequently pictured them as white-washed tombs. Publicly their acts were ceremonial and correct, while inwardly they were filled with pride and prejudice. Jesus knew the untouchable reputation of the prostitutes, thieves, and tax collectors. Nevertheless he sought them out, ate at their tables, and publicly ministered to them with love and tenderness.

Genuine Christianity seeks the highest welfare of mind, body, and spirit of every man. When a Christian is tempted to aloofness, to pride, or to prejudice, he negates the ministry of justice which is inherent in his Christian faith.

A modern prophet, Kahlil Gibran, speaks to this, "Why are you living in the shadow of parasitism, segregating yourselves from the people who are in need of knowledge? Why are you depriving the country of your help? Jesus has sent you as lambs amongst the wolves; what has made you as wolves amongst lambs? Why are you fleeing from mankind and from God who created you?. . . A word of compassion to the weak criminal or prostitute is nobler than the long prayer which we repeat emptily every day in the temple."

Love and justice are two sides of the same coin of faith. Genuine Christianity produces concern for justice in everyday existence. The right expression of Christian love should cause the church member who owns slum property to improve his property and make it decent for human beings. He will not be able to extort impossible rents. Such justice will demand that a Christian in local politics be willing to submit his own actions to right behavior and ethical judgment. Such justice will demand of the missionary-minded churchman concern also for another race in his own community, even before he sends money across an ocean. Such justice will bring insight to the hymns which a Christian congregation sings about brotherhood under God. Such justice will thrust an individual Christian into active roles of Christian action to secure justice for his fellowman. Christian faith expresses the concern that we love one another without distinction of religion, race, color, or class. Christian faith recognizes no special breed of men nor does it overlook any areas where men live and suffer.

The comfort of your pew and the isolation of your narrow world of interests and ambitions sometimes preclude knowledge of a larger world of injustice. It is as though you reside at the top of a pyramid. The vast base of the pyramid is one of anguish, hard toil, and tears, to make it possible for your pinnacle to be secure and easy. Tolstoy questioned, "Is it to know that my security and that of my family, all my amusements and pleasures, are purchased at the expense of misery, deprivation, and suffering to thousands of human beings . . . ?"

Responsibility for justice causes you to ask specific questions. Amos and Isaiah asked the questions in their day. Jesus asked them and gave his life to answer them. Free church pastors asked the questions of liberty and justice in the early days of the United States. Mahatma Gandhi asked for justice in colonial India. Catholic and Protestant missionaries have asked the questions about justice in modern Portuguese Angola, at the risk of expulsion. The Black Sash women of South Africa have dared ostracism and prison to remind their nation of racial injustice. The black sash worn across their simple cotton dresses or their fashionable costumes has been a sign of mourning for their nation's sin against the majority sector of the population. Negroes and Puerto Ricans in Harlem have asked about justice. Negroes in Alabama and Los Angeles have asked. Indians in Arizona and Mexican Americans in West Texas have asked the questions of justice. Coal miners trapped in Appalachian poverty are asking about justice. Slum dwellers in Chicago are asking. The questions have reached crescendo stage, as though a great chorus of voices were joined asking, "Why?"

IS JUSTICE WORTH YOUR LIFE?

Is it worth your life to see love issue in justice? Wherever the questions of justice are raised and wherever restlessness is man's state, change and conflict begin to occur. The changing scene in our own nation only highlights the great revolutionary changes beyond our nation. Our urban areas show monumental changes taking place. The United States is rapidly shifting from rural to urban. The inner cities are filled with people who have drifted from low income farms and racial minorities. Where massive social surgery is indicated, "Band-Aids" are often dispensed. Cities are still dealt with as though they were buildings without people. Massive programs to perfect material functions largely ignore the humanity involved. Ideas, creativity, and compassionate justice are needed even more than money. Money is necessary also. Welfare programs are archaic when they ignore the need for radical action to revolutionize class and economic structures.

To many of our own citizens, as well as to the rest of the world, we appear to be a nation devoted to playing Don Quixote tilting at the evils of the eighteenth century in a world impatient to realize the fullness of the twentieth. It is difficult to feel the pain or the glory of other men. Today's values are often phony toughness, cheap emotion, and casual violence. The powerful acquire more power, and devote themselves to securing the power they have. Therefore power must be challenged by power. When the powerless and the voiceless find ways to express themselves conflict is inevitable.

Social change in Harlem or Alabama or Los Angeles or

Washington, D. C. has come only through blood, sweat, and tears. The tragedy historians will record is that such change has so seldom been achieved through justice born of love.

REACTIONS TO CHANGE

Massive reaction to change usually occurs. The individual Christian disciple needs to understand his own reaction to change. He needs to understand his unconscious attempt to hold to the status quo. What happens in a community where massive challenge comes to poverty, to racial discrimination, or to political and cultural domination by only one segment of the community? Look at yourself in the process also. You may well be involved.

Fear

One reaction to such an attempt of the disinherited to gain power is a reaction of fear. Much that the privileged have treasured as traditional and comfortable seems to be in danger of destruction. Economic self-interests are involved in the fear of change. A conservative reaction usually seeks to preserve as much as possible of the old structures. Another group in the community may rather passively accept that which they know is inevitable. At the same time they are quietly hostile and refuse to be participants in needed change and justice.

Positive Acceptance

At the other end of the spectrum is positive acceptance and participation in social change as an opportunity to provide justice and fulfillment for all the citizens of the community.

Somewhere in this scale of reaction each man finds himself. Differing points of view clash. Social tension occurs. Change in community and political structures and social institutions may come about without conflict, but ordinarily some type of conflict does occur. The risk of conflict is that it may spill over into violence. It may also produce unexpected results and repercussions. However, for change to occur and for justice to be wrought out of injustice, risks must be taken.

Many communities experience the radical change occurring now that patterns of racial segregation and discrimination have been challenged. From the challenge has come slow, if grudging, movement toward inclusion and enrichment of life for minority citizens.

A WAY OF CREATIVE SELF-DISCOVERY

Movements for justice demand courage and wisdom of the contemporary Christian. He must have insight into the alternatives and willingness to throw his weight on the side of justice, regardless of the circumstances. Climactic times of conflict in change can be a seedbed of creativity.

A Christian women's leader found herself in a vulnerable position during the height of Birmingham's 1964 racial troubles. She was a member of the small but influential committee attempting to keep the public schools open following court orders for integration. Threatened by violence and plagued by obscene calls and community ostracism, she later reported that the period had been the most creative in her life. During the long night vigils she was able to produce a thoughtful and inspiring book on spiritual growth.

In the midst of the chaos and violence at the University of Mississippi when the first Negro, James Meredith, was enrolled, a Baptist collegian befriended him. Hostility and harsh criticism were seen on every side. Nevertheless, the collegian in retrospect saw it as the first testing of his maturity. Alan Paton and Trevor Huddleston of South Africa found their involvement in the cause of justice to be a time of personal growth and rewarding understanding of their fellowman. In communities all over the world the Christian who dares to give himself to the cause of justice will not necessarily find the way easy, but he may find himself.

A HARD LOOK AT THE WORLD

Take a hard look now at your world. You are surrounded by persons, families, communities, and structures of society all of which cry out for justice. Conditions of poverty, prejudice, and powerlessness all demand your discipleship. Love in action means justice in life.

Look at poverty, for example. Poverty, USA, is not fiction. You see it in slum doorways. You smell it in garbage-strewn tenement halls. You recognize it in the hopeless faces of people in charity waiting rooms of hospitals. Who are these people? They are the unemployed miner, the ghetto-dwelling Negro, the farm family moved to town, and the beggar in every "wino" district. These are the people characterized by poor health, cultural deprivation, social ostracism, family strain, and no future.

They are scattered through the entire mainstream of American life. Clustered along mountain ridges or in the inner city or in tiny dying villages, they have been mainly invisible. They have been invisible because the sprawling suburbs and the expressways bypass their districts. They may also have been invisible because too many Christians simply decided theirs was not really poverty but only laziness, ignorance, immorality, or welfare graft. While all these may be involved, we deceive ourselves if we so easily dismiss the poor.

Poverty of body and of spirit in our own nation is only one facet. A whole world of human need stretches from our nation, engulfing a population explosion. To walk down any thronged street in Latin America or the Orient is to be overwhelmed by physical want and suffering. Outstretched hands and reproachful eyes mark your passing. If one is lax, however, such human pain can become commonplace. When men in need blend into the scenery, apathy is but an inch away. Only when a man's tears, sweat, and blood fill your eyes and nostrils will you really care. Only when his cries disturb your sleep will you become alarmed. Only when you know he is but one of a deadly structure of poverty and injustice can you be moved to action.

In his penetrating book, *In the Midst of Plenty,* Ben Bagdikian warns: "Humanitarianism isn't practiced so much as administered. Those hostile to enlargement of government function blame the impersonality of modern charity on the intrusion of government. But this intrusion is inevitable. Only tax dollars can provide the food and shelter that keeps an unemployed family alive. It is not the tax dollar that is at fault; it is the tax payer who thinks the dollar is enough. The human heart is still the chief instrument of salvation for those exiled from the larger world."

THE CHURCH AND JUSTICE

Christians seem particularly vulnerable to Bagdikian's charge. Why have the poor at home and abroad been invisible? If "heart" is to be the chief instrument, Christians should provide it. Heart or love which issues in justice is urgent. Government programs to alleviate poverty are necessary but not sufficient in themselves. History provides many lessons where Christians have abdicated their own ministry to persons in need. From Germany's past, Milton Mayer wrote: "The need for bread was great in Germany and the Nazis fed the poor but they fed them without love, and in taking over the feeding they relieved the Germans of the necessity to love one another."

Love and justice call the contemporary Christian to a confession of guilt for and indifference to the consequences of human need. The Christian faith sees in these consequences the wanton destruction of personality and the senseless waste of human resources.

Isolationism?

At times Christian churches are either so isolationist, or so identified with the middle and upper classes that influence with men of need is forfeited. In the congregation also are people who are active participants in the poverty of others. Their own power or prosperity rests upon the continuation of poverty. Such are the slum landlords, the loan sharks, bribable housing and police officials. Jesus pulls no punches in addressing these people: "Inasmuch as ye have done it unto one of the least of these my brethren, ye have done it unto me."

It is precisely in these events where man experiences injustice that we find selfhood and neighborhood closely involved. It is to these persons and events that the Christian disciple is called in acts of justice born of love. Such love and justice are the highest expression of Christian evangelism. Depth evangelism is concerned with the whole man and all the circumstances of his life. Jesus said of his own evangelistic ministry, "He anointed me to preach good tidings to the poor: he hath sent me to proclaim release to the captives, and recovering of sight to the blind, To set at liberty them that are bruised" (Luke 4:18 Phillips).

Activism?

Jesus was talking about more than activity. Activism is often an attempt to conceal from ourselves and from others just how empty we are. Such activism is sterile even if labeled Christian. In many churches and with many Christians mercy is a dead issue. All the energy has been spent on grooming of self. In an hour of churchly pomp and ceremony, Cranmer, the Archbishop of Canterbury, cried out to his people, "Food grows dearer. Do our brothers grow dearer too? No, they freeze and starve beneath our heaven-bent feet!"

FRONTIERS FOR JUSTICE

The incredible and intolerable fact of abundance surrounded by agonizing hunger creates an arena for love and justice. Many contemporary Christians will spend their lives seeking the solutions to this unbelievable fact.

Poverty

Any well-fed American should find it intolerable that so many millions should be crippled in body and in spirit when it is not necessary. The poor must be rescued from being perpetual wards of the welfare bureaucrats, and the courthouse and city hall political machines. Have-nots of other nations must be given the basic elements to fight for survival. Realistic land reform, decent housing, and opportunities for employment may well mean the difference between healthy social revolution and open bloody warfare. There are thousands of geographical and vocational places to begin this work of love and justice. The only real question is whether or not you have what it takes.

Prejudice

Poverty unmistakably calls for Christian discipleship. So do prejudice and the products of prejudice. Segregation, discrimination, ostracism, and physical violence have been the products of a giant river of prejudice which has poured through our nation and through the world from the beginning of time. Prejudice is obstinate and unreasoning. The emotional furor which prejudice creates dims the keenest mind and distorts the most pleasing personality. People otherwise logical and hospitable become demonic under the curse of prejudice. Writing prophetically from Africa in 1955, Laurens van der Post said, "The root (of prejudice) goes deep into each of you as it does into each of us in Africa; the Civil War has vanished from the scene into the wings of history only to go, unseen and unrecognized, raging on over the same issues in the heart and mind of the individual. It is there an honorable peace must first be achieved before the danger will vanish from your land, mine, and the rest of the world. Let us make no mistake about it; this is a world issue. It is the most urgent issue of our desperate age and it needs a dedicated attention to its origin in the invisible soil of our inmost selves if it is not to end in world disaster."

Racism is tearing the fabric of many nations. In our own for years it was poured out in violence toward the American Indian. Television still capitalizes on the early bloodletting by our forefathers. From slavery days to the present, racism has centered upon the Negro. In less dramatic and far-reaching ways, this prejudice has been evidenced in relationships with all minority groups in the nation. The Jew has tasted its bitter fruits. So has the Latin American, whether of Mexico or Puerto Rico.

Other parts of the world experience similar racial and national tensions. In Southeast Asia the Chinese is the hated figure. The history of Central and South America is written in ink drawn from the blood of the encounter between Spaniard and Indian. The ages-long hostility between the Maya and the Spaniard is still seen today in a nation like Guatemala. The white-black struggle of Africa has been high-lighted at times by the terror of the Mau Mau movement or the more recent Congolese wars. Most current is the seething struggle for dominance between white and black in South Africa or Rhodesia.

Prejudice is a terrible and crippling disease. Economic growth, educational and cultural pursuits, human welfare, and spiritual fellowship can all be stifled when prejudice grips a community. The world will never forget Hitler and Nazism and their prejudice and racism. The terrible deaths of millions of Jewish people are an unforgettable reminder of the prejudice. The Sixteenth Street Baptist Church in Birmingham will never forget the Negro children who died in their Sunday school because of prejudice.

Is it dogmatic to affirm that those who hold to race prejudice are living in heresy? They deny the Scriptures, which teach that all, regardless of race, are of one family with God as Father. This commonness of our humanity is a great binding force. The spirit of Christ challenges the distorted images which would blind us to racial and social reality. In a climate of prejudice, the boldness of Christian love affirms full well-being of the object of that love. Neither skin color, nor national origin, nor language, nor customs and culture can be acceptable deterrents to the active quality of that bold love. From that love, justice becomes a reality.

One of the biggest stumbling blocks to justice in the United States continues to be the distorted Negro images that poison communication between people. White men react not so much to Negroes as to their images of Negroes. The images have always been out of focus, and they grow at times even more grotesque. Kyle Haselden has written with insight, "The Negro is not a race, a caste, or a class. The Negro is not a commodity, or a political bloc, or a labor supply. He is not a category of crime, or illiteracy, or immorality; he is not a housing problem, or an educational problem or any other kind of problem. The Negro is a man, with the foibles and frailties, the longings and fears, the hopes and hungers and aspirations of a man. He is an individual, unrepeatable, irreplaceable man who must be met and dealt with in his own right."

To meet this other man from another race and to relate to him as subhuman is to take away the freedom of his personhood. To do so must be considered sin against God the Creator, as well as sin against the man. This is the evil in prejudice, that it would make a man a thing or an object, less than a full man.

In this new day of race relations, in the aftermath of civil rights and voting rights legislation, a new call for love and justice is issued. Peace and harmony have not been automatic. Indeed in many places the lines between the races have hardened. In other places those who thought they were moderately open have discovered the hard core of prejudice which has been layered over by respectability. Little effort is exercised to seek justice in housing, public accommodations, education, and employment. We have merely provided the opportunity for the Negro to seek his rights in all these areas through due process of law. In other words the legal system recognizes justice for minorities, but our hearts are often still closed to them. It is for this reason that love and justice in Christian-discipleship terms are inseparable qualities. Love and justice can be the major forces battling the disease of prejudice.

A concrete situation which confronts the Christian is the need for ample housing without discrimination. Christians are needed who have the patience and skill to work with a racially changing neighborhood. They can help to stem panic, stop block selling of homes, and develop a sense of trust and community. They can confront the real estate business with ethical demands for honesty and refusal to use scare tactics. Property rights, though sacred and necessary, are not the fundamental rights from which all others come. Human rights are basic, and should be universal. They are more basic even than the derivative rights to trade, to assemble, and to speak. First of all, man is man. Only secondarily is he economic man. We make the same mistake the Communists have made if we evaluate man primarily in terms of his property, his production, or his consumption.

Can there be any greater affront to the God of justice than to hold a man responsible for right behavior while at the same time denying to him those institutions by which he comes to understand what civilization is? Can there be a larger sin against God than to hold a man responsible for the labor involved in building a community while denying to him the full freedom of participation in that same community? Can we forget that we have sentenced man to the bondage of life in a filthy ghetto while at the same time calling him irresponsible because he is dirty? Why do we wonder at the confusion bordering on dark violence in the lives of minority-group adolescents when they have been taught to fear, to hate, and to malign themselves from birth?

These questions must involve us more than the emotional ones which have been asked: "Would you want your sister to marry . . . ?" "What will happen to our property values?" and "But this is our way of life and we dare not change it?" By these questions and an elaborate network of myth we have failed to deal with our own prejudice. The myths of superiority and inferiority lead men to incredible acts. The brutalized instincts of men who can believe that other men are animallike in inferiority will condone torture, rape, murder, and the distortion of legal processes to camouflage the crime. George Bernard Shaw well said that people who believe absurdities commit atrocities. Let such prejudice be punctured by an understanding of man which sees our own humanity as made in the image of God, misshapen by egoism and especially by prejudice which would cause us to exalt ourselves by keeping another in an inferior position. The truth of God and of our Christian faith ought to point this out to us.

Love and justice through Christ are concerned about real men. Consequently philosophical abstractions leave us cold in the face of man and his dilemma. Miguel de Unamuno rejected such abstraction: "Neither 'the human' nor 'humanity'. . . but the concrete substantive—man. The man of flesh and bone; the man who is born, suffers and dies—above all, who dies; the man who eats and drinks and plays and sleeps and thinks and wills; the man who is seen and heard; the brother, the real brother. For there is another thing which is also called man, and he is the subject of not a few lucubrations, more or less scientific. He is the legendary featherless biped . . . the social contractor of Rousseau, the homoeconomicus of the Manchester School. . . . A man neither of here nor there, neither of this age nor of another, who has neither sex nor country, who is, in brief, merely an idea. That is to say a no-man. The man we have to do with is a man of flesh and bone—I, you, reader of mine, the other man yonder, all of us who walk solidly on the earth. And this concrete man, this man of flesh and bone, is at once the subject and supreme object of all philosophy, whether certain self-styled philosophers like it or not."

Thus, love and justice penetrate the categories, stereotypes, and myths about man. Justice issues out of love because man is God's creation and man is the "other," the one like us for whom we are both concerned and responsible.

POWER AND ACTION

Responsible discipleship demands keen assessment of the structures which give birth to and maintain poverty and prejudice. Reality insists that you understand status-quoism, economic determinism, class stratification, political machinery, and the lack of power among the disinherited. By disinherited, of course, we mean the victims of segregation and racial minority policies and those trapped in poverty and unemployment. Harvey Cox says, ". . . the powerlessness of oppressed peoples is the key issue. The real illness of the American city today, and especially of deprived groups within it, is voicelessness, the lack of either the readiness, the capacity, or the channels to make their legitimate needs felt throughout the whole system."

Because of this lack of power and voice in the halls of decision, massive community and political organization has become necessary among the groups who have felt the sting of injustice. Reasonable discipleship demands that the Christian give support to attempts to give to the powerless the power to express themselves and to seek redressment for their grievances. Among some, the right and the willingness to vote become of paramount importance. Among others, organization by communities with spokesmen for their cause is a necessity. For others, political realism demands that power among the privileged be met by political power among the underprivileged. Charismatic leaders are needed. They must combine integrity and social passion with the ability to work within the structures of a bureaucratized society.

Power of itself is neutral. Power ranges from persuasion to naked power with no limitations. Thus power among the privileged may be the hidden power of control of votes, buying of voters, foot dragging, and the control of opponents by threat of economic reprisal. Whole segments of our own population, not to mention many other nations, have thus been effectively silenced and kept in line. Justice becomes crucially important for the Christian when he recognizes responsibility to assess power for what it is and to help the powerless find expression.

An important aspect of Christian responsibility is the political organization of the victims of injustice so that they can use their power to change conditions. Dr. John C. Bennett calls Christianity to such responsibility. He suggests first of all that Christian love must seek justice for the neglected and oppressed in our nation and the whole world. Such justice will be both specific as relates to individual man and corporate as it attacks the structures which produce injustice.

Secondly, Dr. Bennett suggests that the church should not choose simply to be a sect made up of a few who belong to a certain class or those who hold to the same opinions or to one racial group. He thus declares the openness of the Christian church. Only the Christian fellowship which has declared its own congregational openness dares to participate realistically in campaigns for justice and open housing, fair employment practices, and adequate and fully integrated schooling.

Openness of spirit is a consistent quality. Where barriers are erected or the mind is closed, the whole consistent framework is thus damaged. Consequently love and justice are costly qualities of discipleship. It is no wonder that individual Christians, as well as congregations, have wrestled with great controversy concerning personal and corporate involvement in the cause of justice. Concern for man, born of Christian love, leaves little room for action which excludes justice.

The life-style of slums and ghettos is apathy. Dormant hostility and inarticulate resentment prevent the people from helping themselves. When individuals or groups historically have attempted to find expression for demanding justice, they have so often been met by cold indifference or even outright violence by the other side that the cause has often been abandoned. Such a day is fast disappearing in our own land and in many of the other lands of the world. The real question is whether or not Christians of compassion, valor, and wisdom shall give themselves to participation and leadership in the movements for justice. If not, the Christian shall that much be diminished by his apathy or cowardice, and the movements of the disinherited shall too often be dominated by bitterness or reactionary hate, as among some "Black Power" leaders.

In the past, social welfare has too often concentrated on symptoms rather than causes. The individual has been seen and dealt with as an individual and the context and circumstance of his life largely ignored. Realistic and massive social justice for today will hit the causes as well as treat the symptoms. The chain reactions of poverty leading to despair, and discrimination leading to cultural deprivation must be explored and thwarted. The Christian is indeed in the right place when, in his own community first of all, he finds both sympathetic response within himself and participation in activity designed to bring justice to all men regardless of race, class, or political stance. He thus brings unique and saving dimensions to the cause. His justice is born not merely of indignation, but of *"agape"* love.

COMPARISON DEDICATED TO WHOLENESS

Justice thus motivated by love is compassionate and dedicated to the establishment of man's wholeness. The Christian's concern for man's salvation is integral to his acts for justice. Man is more than a unit or a tool to be used or manipulated. Man in Christian dimension is not lost in the mass nor sacrificed to the cause. His humanity under God is held inviolable and important.

Christians thus have much to give to the causes of justice. For example, genuine love tunes in to man's despair and man's need. Love hears a man's voice, sees his face, recognizes his condition. Genuine love refuses to cast man in a mold or to deal with him as a robot.

Love listens. Tillich pointed this out: "The relationship of justice to love in personal encounters can adequately be described through three functions of creative justice, namely, listening, giving, forgiving. In none of them does love do more than justice demands, but in each of them love recognizes what justice demands. In order to know what is just in a person-to-person encounter, love listens. It is its first task to listen. No human relationship, especially no intimate one, is possible without mutual listening."

Tillich described, in part, the love Paul admonished in the thirteenth chapter of First Corinthians: "I may speak in tongues of men or of angels, but if I am without love, I am a sounding gong or a clanging cymbal. I may have the gift of prophecy, and know every hidden truth; I may have faith strong enough to move mountains; but if I have no love, I am nothing. I may dole out all I possess, or even give my body to be burnt, but if I have no love, I am none the better.

"Love is patient; love is kind and envies no one. Love is never boastful, not conceited, nor rude; never selfish, not quick to take offence. Love keeps no score of wrongs; does not gloat over other men's sins, but delights in the truth. There is nothing love cannot face; there is no limit to its faith, its hope, and its endurance" (I Cor. 13:1–7 New English Bible).

It is little wonder that many white Americans were dismayed by their inability to cope with the conquering love of Negro Christians during a time of national racial revolution. Even the non-Christian Negroes could not fully understand the power of this love seeking justice among members of their own race. When participants in the nonviolent movement received threats and physical harm, they met these with quiet and determined calmness. Their soft speech and firm but forgiving spirit unnerved the strongest of their antagonizers. The nonviolent way was the perfect way to usher in a movement for racial justice. It was rooted in the New Testament concept of love.

Justice motivated by love also rejects any idea of a half-affluent society. Consequently the movements out of poverty and prejudice have formed a commitment to an equalitarian ethic that may be able to act on a world scale. Coalitions have been formed across racial, class, and economic lines to get at the root causes of injustice. These militant seekers of justice have so often seen hypocrisy in the proclamations of politics that they do not like slogans. They generally prefer to proceed by acts which bear witness to their beliefs rather than by resolutions and public statements about their beliefs. They are increasingly impatient with the mentality that believes time will eventually heal differences and bring more justice.

Their efforts should never be classified as mere faddish enthusiasm. Unquestionably, there are some individuals who like to ride the bandwagon of a new cause. For most, however, there is a vocational commitment to justice. Many of them make no attempt to fall back on their families or their professions for help when the going gets rough.

It is important that the Christian disciple recognize his role as one of wholehearted commitment to the causes which will bring justice out of mass poverty, sectional illiteracy, and patterns of prejudice and discrimination. An occasional slumming trip or an infrequent affirmation of concern for justice is belittling to the faith of one who remembers the cross of Jesus Christ as central event in his faith.

Full freedom and justice for every man is thus a mandate. Recognizing both the ideal and the real, you are challenged to pursue justice, which includes adequate and integrated educational opportunities; no discrimination in training, employment, job promotion, or labor union membership; right to a fair trial; justice and respect at the hands of law enforcement officers; the unhindered right to vote; the right to seek public office; voluntary but free social relationships; and last, but not least, open churches and open religious institutions.

THE CHRISTIAN'S MANDATE FOR JUSTICE

Christian love then has no alternative but to seek justice. A just God demands justice in man and between men. Justice is love's application in a sinful society. It is the behavior and action required now by love, regardless of personal cost. Justice is consistency in belief and behavior. If man is God's creation and more than a thing, then his humanity becomes paramount in all events.

Concern for Justice . . . Regardless of . . .

The Christian thus is concerned not only about the effect of alcohol, narcotics, gambling, and sexual immorality on man and communities of men. With consistency he gives himself to a search for effective justice wherever man is involved. He aligns himself with movements to overrule discrimination in employment, housing, and educational facilities. He seeks just penal codes and asks responsible questions about the justice of capital punishment.

He becomes involved in programs of juvenile correction

and rehabilitation in his own community. He gives himself to the organization of minority groups without representation so that they can express their needs and determinations. He fights corruption in politics, and does not flinch when the politician is a churchman, but pursues justice nevertheless. He seeks to abolish substandard lucrative housing and to make housing more humane. He is concerned about shoddy business ethics, even though the fruits of some business endeavors may end up in church offering plates.

His justice makes no distinctions about the people involved. Neither race, nor national origin, nor station nor class, nor political affiliation are as important to him as seeing justice done. His costly discipleship is expressed as the young German theologian Dietrich Bonhoeffer expressed: "Love asks nothing in return, but seeks those who need it. And who needs our love more than those who are consumed by hatred and are utterly devoid of love? Who in other words deserves our love more than our enemy? Where is love more glorified than where she dwells in the midst of her enemies? Christian love draws no distinction between one enemy and another, except that the more bitter our enemy's hatred, the greater his need of love. Be his enmity political or religious, he has nothing to expect from a follower of Jesus but unqualified love. In such love there is no inner discord between private person and official capacity. In both we are disciples of Christ, or we are not Christians at all. Am I asked how this love is to behave? Jesus gives the answer: bless, do good, and pray for your enemies without reserve and without respect of persons."

Concern for the Injust

Justice born of Christian love not only seeks the well-being of the victims of injustice, but is involved also in a ministry of reconciliation with the promoters of injustice. The uniqueness of Christian discipleship is that the Christian becomes a human bridge between people on both sides of barriers. The Christian allies himself with the victim for the victim's salvation as well as with the perpetrator of injustice for his salvation. Herein is the paradox of contemporary discipleship: You are concerned for justice even while praying for the repentance and well-being of the enemy of justice.

The Christian seeks justice for every man but goes even beyond to express the welfare of each as a fellow under God.

Chapter

6

A Way of Life: Morality

THE NATION'S magazines and secular press have "pulpit-eered" in assessing that a morals revolution is occurring in our nation. Did we need these periodicals to remind us? The bribed athlete, the pregnant, unmarried high schooler, the price-rigging executive, the dues-embezzling labor leader, the slum landlord, the dope addict, and the racist live in our towns and communities. We may or may not know these people by name. Nevertheless we live in this climate of moral rebellion. The voices of the rebellion indicate the tremendous shift in values.

A famous magazine's editor says to a college crowd, "Life was made for living. Enjoy, enjoy! You are not responsible to anyone!"

A student exults, "I can't wait for spring vacation. Good old suds, sex, and sand."

"Our small town paper? We don't read it to find out the news, but only if we got caught!"

A television producer's terse staff memo reads: "More violence and more bosoms!"

A book reviewer writes of a best-selling novel: "This gutter to sewer chronicle out-rapes, out-smears, out-hates most of the other literary roughnecks on the market."

A blatantly sexual commercial promises, "You will want to throw all caution to the wind. So will he."

An oil tycoon boasts to an employee, "I haven't paid taxes in years. Let the poor bloke who can't afford a loophole lawyer do the paying."

A high schooler to her mother, "Don't worry. With the pill there's nothing to fear!"

UPHEAVAL IN VALUE SYSTEMS

The upheaval in value systems is radical. Negativism has been prevalent. Especially noticeable is the no-holds-barred approach of the theater to life situations. Unhealthy sex, hate, violence have been dominant themes, portrayed by despairing characters.

Social disintegration is obvious in American culture. The family and community structures of other years have been fractured by the mobile and rootless nature of the new society. Marriage breakup, the one-parent family, and the rise in numbers of births out of wedlock are quoted in alarming statistics. Gang violence and mugging threaten most city slums. At the same time, pointless destruction of property and growing narcotics addiction have invaded the suburbs.

Mental illness has come to be a national plague. Some estimates indicate one half of the hospital beds in the United States occupied by mental patients. High rates of school dropouts indicate purposelessness. On the other hand, preoccupation with high beginning salaries and fringe and retirement benefits plague upper class youth.

In it all, the hidden persuaders of advertising assure us that certain products will meet man's every need. If he is in a tight spot he can always get a loan from the finance company, if he is low he can light up a well-known cigarette, if he is lonely he can switch on color television, if he has a headache he can use any one of a dozen different kinds of headache relief with or without fizz, and if he is maladjusted he can find the psychoanalyst in the yellow pages.

ASK YOURSELF . . .

"Everybody's doing it" is a commonly heard theme. The emphasis is thus placed on belonging to a group rather than upon the importance of what that group believes and practices. Personal lives are molded by the fashion world, the press, community mores, and status symbols. Augustine affirmed that a community is best described by what it loves and by what it prizes. Apply his formula to your community and to your life. You will find some interesting, perhaps even shocking, conclusions about what you and your community are really like.

For example, how do you spend your time? Your money? Your energy? What are the most popular places in your community? Who are the most popular people? Why are they popular? Who occupies the places of community and political leadership? What kind of men and women are they? How did they become the power structure figures? The answers to all these questions are keenly important in understanding your own sense of values and the values of your culture.

Ask yourself some other exemplary questions which when answered with honesty will give you insight into yourself. Am I a person of habitual honesty in the classroom, on assignments, in the presentation of ideas, with my earnings, in sharing news of people and events? Am I tempted to buy and read pornographic literature? Do the movies labeled "For Adults Only" arouse my curiosity? Do I like to tell obscene stories? Do I tend to follow companions of loose reputation who make my decisions for me? Do I relate the lordship of

Christ to personal sexual conduct, and the sanctity of the body?

Can I evaluate the moral issues involved in politics, community actions, and the speeches and actions of public figures? Do I relate to others as persons regardless of their religion, race, color, or sex? Am I able to affirm their well-being by Christian love through private thought, public statement, and action? These and questions like them are probing. They tend to cut away the layers which cover your real understanding of values.

IS MORALITY ABSOLUTE OR RELATIVE?

One of the most debated issues of the day is whether morality is characterized by absolutes or relatives. Once upon a time the majority of people seemed to think they knew exactly what Christian conduct was. Moralism, rather than morality, may have been involved but nevertheless people generally were rather dogmatic about moral absolutes. Usually in the church, morality meant the denial of certain activities such as dancing, smoking, drinking, card playing, and the theater, with considerable dark aspersions about sex.

Shades of Gray

Today more people recognize that morality is not an easily defined contrast between black and white, but that there is considerable gray shading also. Personal and social morality are obviously interrelated also, and the latter not to be ignored. R. H. Tawney asserted: "To urge that the Christian life must be lived in a zealous discharge of private duties—how necessary! Yet how readily perverted to the suggestion that there are no vital social obligations beyond and above them! To insist that the individual is responsible, that no man can save his brother, that the essence of religion is the contact of the soul with its Maker, how true and indispensable! But how easy to slip from that truth into the suggestion that society is without responsibility, that no man can help his brother, that the social order and its consequences are not even the scaffolding by which men may climb to greater heights, but something external, alien and irrelevant . . . individualism in religion led insensibly, if not quite logically, to the individualist morality, and an individualist morality to a disparagement of the significance of the social fabric as compared with personal character."

Absolutes Are Hard to Find

Obviously a thoughtful person recognizes that there are both personal and social moral issues where absolutes are difficult to find. For example: A doctor takes the Hippocratic oath in which he pledges to do everything within his medical power to extend a patient's life. New drugs, however, make it possible to extend life beyond the point where recovery is either possible or desirable. What should the doctor do?

People should honor their contracts in housing, but when a landlord consistently refuses to make absolutely essential repairs must the tenant keep on paying rent for substandard housing? Wars were once easily classified as just or unjust, but now nuclear conditions make such easy judgments debatable. What is right?

The list of subjects where morality seems relative goes on and on. It is little wonder that considerable discussion is occurring today about standards of morality. Such discussion is healthy but requires thorough thought and conviction.

The current discussion on morality brings together many diverse views. Everything from fundamentalists' moralistic statements to *Playboy's* philosophy is being propounded as the only way in morality. Obviously the Old Testament stone tablets containing the Ten Commandments do not give sufficient help for today. Neither do the taboos of the past century shed light on man's current predicament. At the same time, the other end of the spectrum which insists that all morality is relative leaves considerable room for confusion.

No Code Covers Everything

In the first place the contemporary Christian needs to understand that he is not supplied with a simplistic moral code. There is no handbook of Christian ethics which lists all the problems from alcoholism to cheating to divorce, giving precise answers for each. There is no Christian code which explicitly tells a doctor whether or not to give drugs to a patient with terminal cancer. There is no authoritative word which instructs the youthful citizen whether to be a conscientious soldier or a conscientious objector. There is no ethical code which justifies the time for a rent strike or tells one he ought not to strike. Jesus Christ obviously avoided erecting a rigid code of ethics. Rather he called men to discipleship and to the overwhelming claim of Christian love.

HOW DO YOU FUNCTION MORALLY?

But what does this mean to you when you are caught in dilemmas of magnitude? What do you do when your culture places its stamp of approval upon excessive drinking, or sexual mores condoning premarital intercourse, or rationalization which avows that cheating is all right as long as you don't get caught, or exclusiveness which permits social and racial cliques to discriminate against persons?

Be Consistent

The scene is complicated by the fact that on the other end

of the spectrum those most adamant about the "thou shalt not" sins do not see the immorality of their gossip, slander, pride, hatred, or social irresponsibility. Christian students in Latin America often ask why so much emphasis is placed by some missionaries and national pastors on "giving up" dancing, drinking, and the theater, when little is said about justice. One student asked specifically, "Why not organize against illiteracy, hunger, land control by the oligarchy, political tyranny, graft, and class warfare?" His question is both disturbing and relevant. Personal piety and social morality are not mutually exclusive but consistently related. Consistency in morality is a major question, and probably the major struggle of the contemporary Christian.

Don't Throw Stones

Pride, too, can be a terrible trap. It is easier to find immorality in another. Jesus reminded the stone-throwers about the glass quality of their own houses. The teetotaler immersed in his prohibition activity tends to overlook his own humanity and errors. The political reformer can get so carried away with his programs to abolish corruption that he walks over people as though they were things. The civil rights worker may relish his own sense of involvement and fall prey to a cynical judgmental attitude.

Such blindness tends to characterize many groups in our culture. Some pseudo-patriotic organizations distort the facts and malign persons in the guise of loyalty to nation. Some charities, clubs, and service organizations cover their class and race exclusiveness with deeds of mercy. Some churches avoid attacking the structures of poverty by annual spurts of goodwill in distribution of food baskets. Some governments employ elaborate schemes to make gross immorality palatable to the voters. Both individually and corporately, the entire framework of our culture is riddled with moral inconsistency.

ETHICS IN BUSINESS, POWER STRUCTURES, AND SEX

Before attempting to tackle the basic problem of how one makes ethical decisions, let us explore several areas which give insight into the overall problem. We will look at three particular areas involving moral choice: the business world, the use of power, and the world of sex.

The Business World

The world of business gives innumerable pictures of ethical illness both in management and in labor. Many people seem to feel that these incidents are more unfortunate than they are wrong. Our society often condones or ignores deception, fraud, ruthlessness, and undue regard for narrow self-interests. Nevertheless, it should be recognized that ethical, or unethical, conduct in business is always the conduct of people who are making choices either singly or with others.

Executives of modern business face multiple ethical questions. Should the businessman always look out for the good of the company or for the good of his employees? Should he attempt to find quasi-legal maneuvers to circumvent the tax laws? Does he have enough knowledge about human behavior to make right decisions? Often ethical decisions conflict with a set of principles developed years ago when business was more simple. In the past people could look out for their own private advantages under wide-open competition. Such business encouraged self-reliance and initiative. At the same time it did little to limit the expression of unhampered self-interest. Read about the days of the "robber barons" to get insight into the unlimited power which management was able to exercise.

Now, however, decision making has new dimensions. Social responsibility is stressed. Awareness that the public interest is not served by an uncontrolled marketplace has issued in conscious self-restraint of both individuals and corporations. The government also has intervened to provide the external restraints. Consequently we have moved to a very complex economic life. Organizations at every level—business, communications, transportation, industry—have multiplied. The standard of living has skyrocketed. Labor unions have become very powerful. Government has also grown and continues to curtail the unlimited exercise of business. Government intervenes in the unlimited exercise of power by labor unions. Such large-scale organization is a fact of our day. You will live with this all the years of your life. Concentration of economic power makes possible great achievements, but it also brings the dangers of irresponsible use of power.

Giant organizations are able to exercise power in many ways. They undertake research which may shape tomorrow. They hire and fire large numbers of people. The distribution of wealth is affected through the decisions made in management and labor. Industries are hugh consumers. Even their foreign trade can make or wreck the economy of another nation.

At the same time it should be recognized that corporate bigness is ethically neutral. The real test comes in the question of whether this bigness and its resultant power are used to serve worthy ends. The key ingredient in ethical decisions in this new dimension of bigness then is the conflict which is inherent in what is right and good for numerous groups of people. Modern society includes groups with many conflicting interests. The simple truth is that what may be good for one group may be unfair or even damaging to another. This is especially true in relationships between labor and management. The imperative then seems to be for a business to work toward a maximum appropriation of what is both right and good for all interests after taking all the factors into account. Obviously black-and-white contrasts shade into gray in many such decisions.

For example, what is the purpose of the business organization: to make money or to serve the public interest? How private is private enterprise? What are the public aspects of large corporations?

It is also true that there is a certain system of checks and balances in both small and large contemporary business. The power of a union and the power of a corporation may act as checks on each other. Public regulatory bodies and legislation tend to restrain power also. Internal codes, review boards, and self-evaluation within powerful bodies limit unrestrained use of power. Not to be forgotten also is the power of public opinion. Both labor and management are excessively concerned about their "image."

When individuals or management or labor become involved in kickbacks, payoffs, and manipulation of economies, the whole structure of business is hurt. Distrust is fostered. When officials in a company are guilty of price rigging, all of management falls under suspicion in the public mind. When a labor leader embezzles funds or imposes tyrannical power over the members of a union, all of labor suffers from the notoriety.

Stanley Rowland wrote of one such case: "If the ethical fabric comes apart, the society splinters, or adopts increasing coercion to preserve itself. This danger inheres in unethical economic practices. A good example is Stanley Steinberg. When forced to resign from a subsidiary of Sears, Roebuck

& Co. in 1952, he had $124,000 distributed in twenty-seven banks. This was about half of the total that he took from clothing manufacturers. Moreover, when he moved to a new house he levied manufacturers for a $475 dryer, a custom television set, a gas range, and refrigerator, and other wares. The wife of one manufacturer was made to supply a home cooked turkey when the Steinbergs wanted fowl. Another manufacturer was detailed to take Steinberg's aging parents out to dinner frequently. Steinberg also chiseled stamps, stationery, and cigarettes. 'Nothing,' a district attorney remarked when the reckoning came, 'was too small for Steinberg.' The grid of Steinberg's identity and ethics was open at the end like a big funnel, scooping everything he could, and never satisfied: he even felt driven to chisel his newspapers."

Such cases are unfortunately legion. They operate at every level of management and labor. Pilfering of property and supplies by lesser employees of large businesses has become a major source of loss to business. Who would attempt to catalog the hours lost by laziness, waste, and indifference by millions of employees? Unethical practices and decisions riddle the whole structure.

In the face of corporate bigness and the need for ethical decision making, are there claims which Christ makes of his disciples? How should the Christian act as a decision maker? Christian faith affirms that God does act in social structures. God's claims for faithful obedience touch all men who work in the power complex of today.

The Christian may know that the God for whom he decides is present and active in the world of business structures where men work. Consequently decision making in ethics stresses competence, information, and responsibility. Good intentions are not enough. Decisions must be rooted in fact, compassion, and keen awareness of the circumstances.

The Christian gospel is relevant in a society where social responsibility is a requirement.

Structures of Power

Moral discipleship in the realm of business and power complexes is concerned with man and his well-being. In the complexity of the modern age man is easily lost to sight or relegated to an inferior position. In industry he becomes a cog. In education he can become a parrot. In totalitarianism, a puppet. In science, a formula. Particularly in a cybernetics age morality is important in reminding men and power complexes that man is over the machine. The fantastic accomplishments of the age of automation defy imagination. One giant United States corporation is able to program its entire production, inventory, and engineering problems from eighty-five different factories and plants through one computer brain located in the heart of the nation.

Jacques Ellul has predicted that by the year 1975 half of American industry will be producing things not yet invented today. By 2000, travel to the moon will be commonplace and men will inhabit artificial satellites; foods will be synthetic, hence abundant; disease and famine will be abolished; and energy from the sun and the sea will be plentiful. Knowledge will be accumulated in electronic banks and transmitted to the human brain directly by coded messages. There will be no need to study; a person will simply plug in his mind to the computer which instantaneously informs him whatever he needs to know. This surpasses science fiction. Computers will be able to recognize handwriting and the human voice and to transcribe either into written form, as well as to translate languages. When such computers and machines are coupled, all you will have to do is scribble a note in English and have it typed neatly for your friend in Athens, Greece in Greek.

Or you will be able to pick up your phone, dial Buenos Aires, speak English, and the party there will hear your conversation in Spanish as you hear his in English.

Obviously moral choices enter a profoundly new dimension in the age of the machine and the computer. New areas of choice and decision will have to be explored. It is important therefore for you to know the source of morality. The old codes of legalism simply leave one half naked in a cold new world of complexity.

At the same time Christians should not be frightened of the machine, but rather grateful for it and willing to use it responsibly. Robert H. Hamill gave an insightful evaluation of the machine in a speech before the Pacem in Terris Conference in New York City in March of 1965. He said, "With all its spectacular powers the machine makes it possible for men to 'subdue the earth . . . hold dominion over all created things'; therefore we give thanks to the machine for automation, for the cybernated processes. There is nothing inherently wrong with affluence and efficiency in themselves. If God is in the world, he is in the world of machines. In biblical times sheep and vineyards were valid figures of speech about God; today missiles and factories do just as well. The potter's wheel and carpenter's bench of yesterday become the laboratory, the library, and the computer of today. No, Christian suspicion of the machine is not about affluence, but about its overwhelming pride that builds towers to heaven, its distorted worship of its own products (creatures instead of the Creator), its avaricious spirit, its furnishing the nations with torturous and suicidal weapons, its grasping of power and tyrannical influence upon life, its tendency to dehumanize." Hamill sees the moral problems involved for men and structures of men in business and power complexes. The ultimate question will be whether the machine was made for man, or man for the machine.

As you face vocational choices, goals for your life, and relationships to business, labor, and government in powerful structures, your own sense of morality becomes greatly important. If you are a teacher, your preparation and grasp of knowledge become a power to be distorted or used responsibly for the good of your students. If you are a scientist your knowledge and investigative potential become a power to be used either for evil or for good. In the realm of government the same moral use of power and influence has long-reaching effect upon the lives of others. If you are a businessman, quick profits and cutthroat competition can mean the destruction of individuals and other businesses. The incredible power of business allied with government in the whole defense industry is presenting new questions of morality. The temptation is to see wars maintained at a certain pace in order to keep the economy of the defense industry growing. The morality involved in profits made at the expense of human life is a giant specter over our nation. Your moral choices about power and its use thus become very important.

"Everywhere man's power is in unbroken ascendency," said Romano Guardini. ". . . Indeed, we might contend that his power has only now entered upon its critical stage . . . Nevertheless, essentially, the will of the age is no longer directed to the augmenting of power as such. . . . In the coming epoch, the essential problem will no longer be that of increasing power—though power will continue to increase at an even swifter tempo—but of curbing it. The core of the new epoch's intellectual task will be to integrate power into life in such a way that man can employ power without forfeiting his humanity. For he will have only two choices: to match the greatness of his power with strength of his humanity, or to surrender his humanity to power and perish." Here

Christian discipleship enters decisively. The capacity to be a man of Christ, with commitment to morality, will bring answers. For one thus helped and fortified, the strength of his humanity is equal to the monstrous power set over against him.

Sex

Let us move now, however, to another area where man's frailty involves making numerous moral choices. The world of sex is very much with us. This is a sex-affirming age. The pendulum swings audaciously from Victorian prudishness to the "Playboy" notion of sex as status. Where sex was once a deep dark secret, it has become a blatantly announced commodity.

Undoubtedly social mobility and urban anonymity have played large roles in the change. As people have moved from rural to urban situations, they have readily slipped away from the small town's moral code. The anonymity in metropolitan life makes one less inhibited in his sexual conduct. Drama, art, and literature have all contributed toward giving sex a platform from which to speak.

Unapologetically it can be said that some of the shift is healthy. Sex needed to lose its subterranean, other worldly atmosphere. Children for generations have encountered their own sexual appetites without proper information and counsel to enable them to relate normally and healthily to others. Parent-child communication often found itself most stymied at the point of sex. Storks and birds and bees were made to carry fascinating secrets of which the precocious child was contemptuous.

At the same time it should be said that there are gross myths about sexual morality in today's culture. To some current spokesmen on sexual morality, the individual has complete freedom to function sexually as long as he believes what he is doing is proper and acceptable. Such a loose structuring seems little more than a disguise for pleasure and a rationalization for breaking the old taboos.

Another myth says that sex is a completely private and personal matter. This is a myth because sex, in reality, goes beyond the private. The relationship of two persons in sex may form a chain of circumstances involving many persons. The birth of a child out of wedlock, for example, is more than a private matter.

Another myth carried over from past generations consists mainly of taboos about sex. Much misinformation, threat, and evil cloud the issue of sex, making it seem abnormal and ugly. Consequently many young people face the most beautiful of human relationships with such giant distortions that years of marriage are warped by the myth that "sex is dirty."

Another common myth is that one is justified in going contrary to his personally accepted moral standards as long as a majority of others are doing the same thing. The old theme "Everybody's doing it" is heard on all sides. Ascertaining rightness or wrongness of action is left to the crowd whose value system one has adopted.

There are serious problems involved in this attitude. Waldo Beach writes: "If the crowd be taken as the final authority, then 'anything goes' when the crowd isn't looking, or when some riffraff in the crowd take over. But a real sense of conscience appears when one acts with integrity in a private unproctored setting, where nobody is watching from the crowd, and where the only being to whom one is responsible is a transcendent Lord who 'looketh on the heart.' Christian integrity is conscience which seeks to be responsible to the will of God, and is therefore the same in private life as in public." The crowd often is taken as the authority in making decisions because of concern with acceptance and status. What a splendid trap snobbery can be, however. The current phenomenon of mass society is responsible for many a person being lost in the crowd or overwhelmed by it.

Another common myth about sex is that you can always control it. It is true that either you control sex or it controls you. Nevertheless passion and temptation often overrule logic and vision of the consequences. You have probably been involved in an experience where you promptly said to yourself, "That was not me. How did it happen? It seemed as though I were someone else." Most people have the feeling at times of being Dr. Jekyll and Mr. Hyde. Within the person the balance between the tendency toward right and the tendency toward wrong is delicate indeed. We are wont to shift responsibility for our wrongdoing and even for our temptations. Let's face it, however. We are led astray by our own desires. At times we deliberately, premeditatedly enter into actions which are wrong. Although temptation may come from outside ourselves, there is at the same time that within us which responds to it. The responsibility for our action is ours. We make our own decisions. Our wills are ours with which to say "Yes" or "No."

These myths only point up the wide variety of historic and cultural response to sex relationships. The Victorian era proclaimed a love without sex. Human love was an abstraction, an ethereal quality divorced from the natural functions of the sex relationship. Consequently sex was given a darkly mysterious quality. Because it was spoken of in hushed tones, all sex took on an air of evil in the minds of the majority.

Today these Victorian roots still grow in the new soil of more openness with regard to sex. At the same time the picture has only been reversed in what is widely proclaimed as the openmindedness of the "Playboy" philosophy. While openmindedness is important, this philosophy is but turning the coin over to see sex without love. The relationship is thus proclaimed as a purely physical alliance without ultimate responsibility to the other party involved.

Harvey Cox adequately dissects this basically anti-sexual concept. Cox says that the "Playboy" philosophy is an attempt to give a total image of what it means to be a man. The wide reception the philosophy has received is probably rooted in the loss of understanding of what it means to be male or female. Traditional roles of male and female have shifted so in the modern age that what was once understood as maleness has changed. The "Playboy" philosophy attempts to restore a new and modern image. Sex is proclaimed to be an item of leisure activity and the girl is but the accessory in this recreational pursuit. This "anti-sex" feeds on the existence of a fear, perhaps repressed, of involvement with women in the long haul of marriage. The concept fosters heresy in the understanding of what a person is. The person is seen as a body or a thing for the gratification of sexual desires. The moment of pleasure is seen as all important. What happens beyond to the emotions and thought processes of the individual is unimportant. Sex is thus seen as little more than an animallike bodily gratification.

Sex in our culture is defined variously. It is a commercial asset to be exploited. It is recreation. It is a weapon to use against another person. It is a cure for loneliness. It is a stolen pleasure. It can be a status symbol for the wealthy. It is often equated with romantic love. All such definitions miss the mark of reality of the gift of sex. Sexual impulses are basic and powerful. There are other impulses also which can be closely aligned with sex and can mean real trouble. There are the impulses to win approval, to achieve, to gain revenge, to have security, and to gain power. Coupled with an unrealistic view of sex these impulses can ruin your life. Sex denied or pursued for selfish ends breeds frustration and despair as well as aggression. Promiscuity usually involves lying and taking advantage of another. Sex is thus divorced from the person and from any sense of tenderness. Complete social irresponsibility is involved in aggressive sex.

Cutting through all the wrong definitions, the abuses and fallacies of sex, is the Christian concern for the personhood of the individual. We have seen this theme running through most of the areas we have discussed. Christian love seeks to promote the highest welfare of the object of love. Here then is built-in help for making moral choices in the area of sex. The choice really lies between immaturity and maturity. When sex is involved, a long look must be taken. The choices will bear upon either a positive or a negative preparation for marriage and parenthood. Sex is the relationship of two persons, more even than of two bodies. The commitment of oneself to another is involved. The enjoyment of sex within this dimension is the only enjoyment that makes sense. The enjoyment that ignores the future has no future. Its unreality makes it little more than a form of temporary escape.

WHAT DOES IT MEAN TO BE MORAL?

Here then we have had glimpses into some of the problems and decisions confronting us in the area of business, power, and sex. What does it mean then to be a moral person?

Struggle and Discovery

First of all, morality is the fruit of one's personal grappling with life through Christian commitment, rather than conformity to a legalistic code. Obedience to the past is not as important as struggle and discovery in the present.

It is thus important to make a careful distinction between

morality and moralism, and between authority and authoritarianism. Moralism distorts moral principles by making them rigid systems of conformity. Taboos tend to displace concern for Christian growth, urging only unquestioning obedience. Persons who do not thus conform to the rigid standards are considered outcasts. Such a concept makes of man little more than a robot performing to the dictates of a giant divine morality computer. The authoritarian-moralistic concept of morality is primarily external and is fed by implied threat and force.

This criticism should not keep you from understanding the worth of legal and social sanctions which help to define and control human behavior. At the same time authentic Christian ethics is not legalism. Waldo Beach says, "It is not a catalogue of do's and don'ts. This impression about Christian ethics is widespread in a church culture. Should you ask the average layman about his conception of what it means to be a Christian, his answer would be a series of things a Christian does—or more likely does not do—virtues displayed and sins abhorred. Legalism of this sort defines the Christian life in outer and plural ways and is no different in essence from the Pharisaism of the New Testament period. . . . Vital Christianity is constantly at war with a tendency within itself toward legalism. Authentic Christian ethics is inward and dynamic, dealing in the realm of tensions and motives, 'the heart.' It cannot decide ahead of time, as does a rule book, what is to be done or not done, for weekends or weekdays. It cannot prescribe the content of decision. It can only prepare for decisions, which must be freshly and freely made in each new situation." Morality is thus seen as more than mere shallow obedience to a rigid system.

Growing Understanding of Commitment

In the second place, morality is a growing understanding

of commitment rather than a set code of conduct. It is not static but flexible, recognizing that Christian conduct must differ in differing circumstances. In other words, man is not like white rats which can be programmed as in scientific research nor does he respond as Pavlovian dogs would to certain stimuli. Man is man. He seeks to respond in Christian discipleship to the living God in life situations. Indeed he gets help from what men did in a past generation. He gets tremendous insight into ethical decisions from Old and New Testament Scriptures. He gets inspiration for making the right choices from the high principled and courageous actions of men of other days. Nonetheless, he still must face his own life situation and his peculiar set of circumstances. Because life shifts, cultures change, and science is not static, man finds himself with new situations challenging his integrity and his wisdom to act rightly. He is guided by principles, and he is also guided by consequences. His choices act as a bridge between his past and his future. He can take several directions in the future. His choices thus give his life shape and direction. When he proceeds rightly he grows in maturity and helps make society around him more sound. The highest ethical need of man is to use his free choices to shape a positive direction for life.

CHRISTIAN ELEMENTS IN DECISION MAKING

To ask specifically, "Is it right to ——? Is it wrong to ——?" is necessary, but may at the same time be premature or even superficial. One cannot find packaged answers for all the specifics of life even though our natural inclination is to seek them. Flexibility in Christian morality rather means that one is guided first by his relationship to Christ. Out of that relationship emerge Christian elements in decision making. Obviously there could be many such elements but three have special merit.

God Judges All

First, the Christian disciple sees all the events, persons, situations, and systems of his life and his world as under God's judgment. In other words, no one political party holds ultimate truth in its grasp. No one economic system is the last word. Neither labor nor management is greater than God's judgment upon each. God transcends communities and their mores and ideals—in business, politics, and sex.

This means that all your practices, your habits, your causes, and your ideals are to be judged by God. You are ultimately accountable to him. Your immorality results then from a disordered relationship with God which usually disorders your relationship with your fellowman. Your immorality results from placing some object, event, desire, goal, or person in that highest place of accountability reserved to God's judgment. You thus trust in something other than God's purpose for your life. You love in some way other than God's intention for human relationships.

God Loves All Men

In the second place, in grappling with moral choices you must be aware of God's love for all men without respect of person. To know that this love encompasses your enemies, your friends, your associates, your competitors, your neighbors, and every other person beyond your life sobers you in your actions and reactions toward each. This overwhelming understanding of love as the highest motivation requires you to ask: What does this love expect of me? Am I willing and able to serve the needs of others and to affirm their personhood? The scriptural word is plain: "We love because he loved us first. But if a man says, 'I love God', while hating his brother, he is a liar. If he does not love the brother whom he has seen, it cannot be that he loves God whom he has not seen" (I John 4:19-20 New English Bible).

You thus go beyond the old legalisms, taboos, and prohibitions because something higher is required. A more meaningful, and at the same time, more human way of morality is involved. It is as old as the life and teachings of Jesus Christ, but as new as today's most exacting situation. Jesus was asked, "Master, which is the greatest commandment in the Law?" He answered, " 'Love the Lord your God with all your heart, with all your soul, with all your mind.' That is the greatest commandment. It comes first. The second is like it: 'Love your neighbour as yourself.' Everything in the Law and the prophets hangs on these two commandments" (Mat. 22:36–40 New English Bible). Morality is thus the fruit of inner faith. It is the way of profound love. It can never be a mere program of self-improvement nor adherence to a code of ethics.

But perhaps you are saying, "I don't have what it takes." Only a moral superman could so live. The demands are too strong. The times are too immoral and too tough. You may simply wish to evade asking, "What is right? What is just?" But you cannot if you have set your course in Christian discipleship. Jesus was no starry-eyed dreamer. He was not ignorant of the frailties of man. He knew the relativities of our choices. Moffatt translates: ". . . he . . . required no evidence from anyone about human nature; well did he know what was in human nature" (John 2:24–25). He knew men could lie, cheat, steal, hate, and kill, yet he called men to discipleship. The call to discipleship today involves morality. Far more is involved than a built-in compass, or the homing instinct of a pigeon, or a kind of intuition about what is right. What *is* involved is the claim of Jesus upon the one who calls him Lord of Life. We shall be judged by the way we live, relate to man, and make our moral choices in the light of that claim of lordship which makes us his disciples.

Chapter

7

The Price to Pay:
Involvement

THE AIRPLANE was at 28,000 feet over the northern coast of South America. I was enjoying the second course of a luxurious meal. Suddenly the food caught in my throat as it dawned on me how easily one shifts gears from concern to aloofness. Just a few minutes before boarding the plane I had driven through some of the worst slums on the continent at the outskirts of Caracas, Venezuela. Hillsides of hovels had been thrown together with pieces of flattened tin cans, rotted timber, and cardboard. Everywhere were the evidences of brutalized life. Now at a safe distance and a safe altitude from reality, those tragic scenes had already slipped from consciousness.

This is a parable of life. You do not have to jet away from the earth to be aloof from it. You can live surrounded by pain, suffering, and tyranny and be a pocket of neutrality. Whether your address is the Caracas slums, or Johannesburg with its "apartheid," or New York's Harlem, or Mississippi's tent cities, or the most fashionable suburbs of San Francisco, Atlanta, or Philadelphia, you may still be out of touch with the reality of life around you. The college students of another generation used to sing a little ditty, "We're here because we're here because we're here because we're here." The words sound suspiciously like the theme song of many a life today.

In the pilgrimage which leads through truth, repentance, courage, love, and justice, the price of life is implicit: involvement. The pilgrimage is a mixture of joy and pain. Christian love repudiates injustice and prejudice. The search for truth disturbs mental stagnation. Moral courage kills crowd-pleasing conformity. An informed vision tears down narrow provincial walls surrounding life. If life thus is to come alive for you, you must plunge yourself into it as a committed follower of Christ. J. H. Oldham says, "There are some things in life, and they may be the most important things, that we cannot know by research or reflection, but only by committing ourselves. We must dare in order to know. Life is full of situations to which I can respond not with part of myself but only with the commitment of my whole being."

You do not learn about human relations only through psychological study. Nor do you learn to swim simply by reading books of instruction. Space cannot be explored only by assertions about what might be found in space. A parachutist never knows the exultation of the jump merely by hearing other chutists relate their experiences.

LIFE IS COMMITMENT

You must take the jump to know the thrill of life. You must relate to man to know him and to appreciate him. In the face of problems, tyranny, human need, and challenge,

you have to ask, "What can I do?" If you would be free to
serve you must cut the ropes that bind and inhibit you. The
ropes may be cowardice, apathy, or greed. Your own salvation and fulfillment are involved.

Albert Camus told the tragic story of a French lawyer
who hears the screams of a drowning woman as he crosses
a bridge late one night. He refuses to risk his own life and
submits himself thus to the tyranny of that awful memory
for the rest of his life. Years later in his ramblings to himself he says, "Tell me what happened to you one night on the
waves of the Quays of the Seine and how you managed never
to risk your life. You yourself utter the words that for years
have never ceased echoing through my nights and that I shall
at last say through your mouth: 'Oh young woman, throw
yourself into the water again so that I may a second time
have the chance of saving both of us!' " Suppression of
commitment to life kills character, haunts the mind, and
poisons life. It is not that we lack the resources to grapple
with the challenges of today, but rather that we lack the will
to use the resources.

You cannot simply change the world or speak to human
events from the outside. Counsel means little when it is
given from the comfortable to the uncomfortable. Criticism
from the grandstand falls on unhearing ears in the arena.
You must get inside. Whether it be an organization, a social
structure, an institution, or the events of human encounter,
you must be willing to be a vulnerable part of those things
in order to give aid. The restlessness which you feel in your
bones must be channeled and articulated. The choices of
what you do with your mind, your body, your preparation,
and your vitality reveal everything about you. Your beliefs
and your values are seen best in terms of what you do with
your life.

SPEAK UP!

The price of involvement is the price of articulating your beliefs. What you believe about God, faith, and discipleship must be expressed by word and by action. Your words and your actions can be a bucket of cold water on a sleeping church. The fact that your faith and your life are linked in vocational commitment speaks volumes.

A student night program audience in a Tennessee church listened with astonishment to a Costa Rican student's affirmation of Christian faith. The local young people present could not forget the unique way the Costa Rican youth was able to express his Christian faith in terms of the goals for life and vocation which he was pursuing. With little English and no money, he had come to the United States to complete a medical education. His grasp of philosophy and theology depicted his spiritual hunger. His concern for his own people without doctors in rural areas expressed the tension of his life which would take him back to his own land. Who he was, what he must do, and where he would go were questions which unified his life. He stood in stark contrast to the drifters and the apathetic among both the older hearers of that congregation and the students.

DO SOMETHING!

Genuine faith is never disembodied. Faith pours out in action, vocation, and commitment. The faith which recognizes that we are created in God's image knows that we must therefore be creative and redemptive in our lives. The Christians who are able to be creative and redemptive make indelible impressions on others around them.

Immediately following the cessation of war with Japan in the 1940's, a Japanese student enrolled in a Texas university. Pearl Harbor was still too painful a memory and "dirty

Jap" was too common an expression for him to escape un-
touched. He had, however, already made his peace with
the cruelty and enmity of men. Transferred with his family
from their California home following Pearl Harbor, he had
known the bitterness of life as a virtual prisoner in an Arkansas detention camp for Nisei. In his teens he had come with
his family to make his home in the United States. Caught
soon after in the tides of war, he had felt the prejudice and
hate which war produces between peoples. Although a loyal
citizen, he was suspected of being an enemy. His bitterness
knew no bounds. His faith in the old gods of his ancestors
had long since diminished.

He found Christian faith in hostile surroundings, however, through the ministry of an Arkansas pastor. The pastor
dared the ostracism of his little town in order to visit the
camp and minister to the Japanese located there. The youth
was suspicious at first but was soon captivated by a man's
faith poured out in love and justice for dislocated people. The
faith of the Japanese youth was built on repentance and forgiveness. His own sense of forgiveness made it possible for
him to forgive those who hated and mistrusted him. Little
wonder then that when he began his university studies he
was able to accept, love, and help students around him. The
demonstration of his own meaningful experience with Christ
touched student's lives and stretched their tiny worlds. He
challenged the stereotypes and prejudices of his fellow students. His own experience of cynicism and of suffering
helped him to understand these qualities in others. He
literally performed a ministry of reconciliation.

RECONCILIATION

Contemporary discipleship involves reconciliation. There
is no such thing as aloof love. In *The Brothers Karamazov*

Dostoyevsky wrote, "I love humanity, but I wonder at my-self. The more I love humanity in general, the less I love man in particular. In my dreams I have often come to making enthusiastic schemes for the service of humanity and per-haps I might actually have faced crucifixion if it had been suddenly necessary; and yet I am incapable of living in the same room with anyone for two days together." Here is where commitment is radically challenged. You are called as a disciple to cross all the barriers which exist between man and man. These barriers may be race, class, caste, language, politics, or nation. Your discipleship zeros in on tension, antagonism, conflict, or injustice. Your reconciling efforts are called for within family groups, in neighborhoods, be-tween races, between political ideologies, between labor and management, and between nations.

When we should have had a corps of St. Francises comb-ing the earth to bind up the wounds of man, instead we have had camera-strung tourists in every major city of the world taking pictures of other people's poverty. Where we should have had doctors, teachers, agricultural specialists and social workers, we have had generals and soldiers instead. When energies should have been expended in aiding minority groups and healing racial conflicts, instead energies were spent in Ku Klux Klans, White Citizens Councils, and other extremists groups. Paul writes to modern-day Corinthians: "From first to last this has been the work of God. He has reconciled us men to himself through Christ, and he has en-listed us in this service of reconciliation. What I mean is, that God was in Christ reconciling the world to himself, no longer holding men's misdeeds against them, and that he has en-trusted us with the message of reconciliation. We come therefore as Christ's ambassadors" (2 Cor. 5:18–19 New English Bible).

Risk

Risk exists, of course, in being such "ambassadors." The risk is in learning to care too deeply. The risk is in involvement. Christian groups need to be stung with such concern. Too few bridges have been built between men. Too few voices have been lifted in the name of Christ calling for love where only hate has ruled. Too few ambassadors of Jesus Christ have opened negotiations between the non-communicating factions of a community or between nations.

The charge has often been laid at the door of the church that it is ascetic, withdrawn from reality. This may be true of churches but it was not true until the church got beyond the New Testament. During the days of New Testament Christianity the charge could not have held water. It ought not to today. In Jesus Christ the church reached out to embrace even the ugliest and most distasteful of men and events in order to redeem them. A healthy faith will accept without fear the hazards of maximum involvement in the world's travail. This is the reason the church of Jesus Christ, and you as an individual Christian, must be present as "salt" and "light" in the human situation.

"Reconciliation" vs. "Evangelism"

Reconciliation may be a more meaningful and responsible term than the common churchly term of "evangelism." Evangelism in depth is interested in the scattering of the church of Jesus Christ into all the spiritual deserts where people live and work: the inner cities, the suburbs, the industrial complexes, the apartment structures, and the expanding university campuses. Yet, constantly, churches are moving away and leaving these same places of ministry. One suspects such churches of attempting to preserve class structure, racial integrity, or financial health. Vacant buildings, closed doors, snobbishness in membership, clublike elegance, and stereotyped ministry must all be an offense to God.

Admittedly, reconciliation is a burden. Consequently Christians fluctuate between narcissism and "scapegoatism." Some Christians spend far too much time on the analyst's couch. They are long on diagnosis but short on therapy. More past sins and failures are dredged up than could be handled in three lifetimes. Brain picking and hand wringing by themselves are dead-end streets.

On the other hand, other Christians have been loathe to admit the need for self-examination. Rather than honest critique of self, they are given to analyzing others. The Ecumenical Movement, the Federal Government, communism, some other nation, or some local theological "heresy" comes under their scrutiny. There should be a happy balance between diagnosis and therapy. Repentance and forgiveness must issue in reconciling witness.

Crossing Barriers

Reconciliation means crossing barriers. Van Cliburn and Benny Goodman have had incredible success in bringing understanding of Americans to the people of Russia. Missionaries have crossed barriers for years to proclaim the radical gospel of the individual worth of man. So radical was their proclamation in Portuguese Angola that many were expelled. They were accused of fomenting revolution by communicating to the Angolans that they were free men under God and should exercise their humanity.

The Missionary and Reconciliation

Particularly in developing nations, the role of today's missionary is changed but still important. The responsible missionary communicates his faith in the language of the people. He has a larger ecumenical spirit of fellowship than do most Christians in the United States. He sees the sense-lessness of competition and exclusivism.

He has battled his own prejudices and come to a genuine and equalitarian love. He has unique insight into minority groups, their concerns, and their needs. He tends probably to over-identify with minority groups in his own land when on furlough. He may make unpopular statements about the need for relevant religion as expressed in human relation-ships, particularly in the racial order. He has discovered al-ready for himself what it means to be a member of a minority group. He knows that only as national leaders emerge is there any real hope for the life of the church. He is able to stand patiently to the side and watch national leaders try their own wings.

He does not use American money as a threat. He does not set himself up as an overlord simply because he is an American, or white, or monied. He is eager to see the cre-ative expression of the Christian faith in the life of the emerging churches to which he relates in another land. He is eager for the development of creative expression in archi-tecture, music, worship forms, religious education, and evangelism. He is a Christian bridge between nations, races, and ideologies. He is a personal incarnation of Christian faith and compassion.

Reconciliation is integral to modern-day missions. Man lives in a revolutionary world experiencing loneliness, mean-inglessness, and depersonalization. He does not give these titles to his feelings nor to his predicament, but they are descriptive of him. Reconciliation—man to God, man to self, man to man—is the greatest task on the world scene for in-dividual Christian involvement. One Latin American critic aptly describes much Christian disengagement from the task of reconciliation. He says that many Roman Catholics are so priestly and conservative in Latin America and concerned about maintaining the status quo that they fail to recognize the revolutionary atmosphere. The Protestants, he says, are so pietistic and wrapped up in North American forms of church life that they cannot translate the gospel into contemporary meanings. Indeed our divisions are great and our misunderstandings are monumental.

A ministry of reconciliation is a sounding of hope. Communism has challenged the disinherited of the world who believe that they will have opportunity for participation in man's freedom. American Christians may have sinned most by proclaiming a gospel of goods, gadgets, and services rather than concepts of equal justice, dignity, and human worth.

The ministry of reconciliation must be more than that from the haves to the have-nots, or from the educated to the illiterate, or from the superior to the inferior. Reconciling Christian witness in Japan must call for faith to be communicated in Japanese raiment in the midst of their shattered ancestral religions. Christian witness in Vietnam must call for hope in the midst of war crisis, and without relating that hope to American soldiers. Reconciling Christian love in Africa must witness in a spirit of equality while repentant at the same time about the obvious lack of such love and equality at times in the United States.

Begin at Home

Reconciliation across racial and language barriers begins first at home, however. Every university campus and major metropolitan center in the United States has resident foreign students. They come from most of the countries of the world and although in our nation only briefly, carry away to their own countries either positive or negative insights into American life.

The price of your discipleship and concern for men of
other nationalities begins in involvement with international
students. They face a battery of difficulties. Some of them are
plagued by insufficient financial support. Others have very
poor early orientation and guidance in the customs and ways
of United States life. Many lack involvement in depth in
either the university or the local community. They have
limited and superficial contact with American families.

Others have immense language difficulties, though some
of them put the average American to shame with their grasp
of vocabulary and accent. Others have difficulty in acquiring
academic training in the United States which will prepare
them for specific jobs in their own country. There are
housing limitations, and in some places, monumental prejudice. International visitors are plagued at times by cliquish-
ness. They are thrown together in self-defense for the
friendship denied them by many Americans.

They suffer at other times from a sense of indifference to
their interests and talents on the part of Americans. They
often feel that they are told more than they are asked about
their own insights and backgrounds. An area of ministry is
ripe for Christian disciples among the growing number of
international guests in our country.

Obviously reconciliation has many faces and many opportunities.

SHARING

Yet another aspect of the discipleship of commitment is
sharing. To share your life, your talents, and your future is to
cast your lot with man for the sake of his redemption. The
day after Bonhoeffer knew he would undoubtedly be exe-
cuted by the Nazis, he wrote in his prison journal: "During
the last year or so I have come to appreciate the 'worldliness'

of Christianity as never before. The Christian is not a homo religiosus, but a man, pure and simple, just as Jesus was a man, compared with John the Baptist anyhow. I don't mean the shallow this-worldliness of the enlightened or the busy, comfortable or the lascivious. It is something much more profound than that. Something in which the knowledge of death and resurrection is present. I believe Luther lived a this-worldly life in this sense. . . . It is only by living completely in this world that one learns to believe. One must abandon every attempt to make something of one's self, whether it be a saint, a converted sinner, a churchman (the priestly type, so called!), a righteous man or an unrighteous one, a sick man or a healthy one. This is what I mean by worldliness—taking life in one's stride, with all its duties and problems, its successes and failures, its experiences and helplessness. It is in such a life that we throw ourselves utterly into the arm of God and participate in his sufferings in the world and watch with Christ in Gethsemane. That is faith, that is metanoia, and that is what makes a man a Christian. How can success make us arrogant or failure lead us astray, when we participate in the sufferings of God by living in this world?"

Bonhoeffer's interpretation is significant. True Christians are the truest humans. Their Christianity is earthy, human, full of life. The Christian does not panic when he confronts pain, terror, or filth in life around him. He recognizes that this could also be his lot. So he casts himself in Christ's name into a sharing of that life so that it might be transformed. He refuses to be cloistered as a separate religious body. He attempts to communicate his faith in God in ways understandable to the unbeliever. He knows his own failure and evil and loves his fellowman who is evil. He yearns to help, to comfort, even to suffer.

Through Lay Service Organizations

It is for this reason that many Christians find themselves magnetized by the work of the Peace Corps, the VISTA programs, and many lay organizations for service at home and abroad. A youth volunteer in the War on Poverty program overheard a seventeen-year-old recruit in a job retraining camp say, "I thought this might be my last chance to make anything at all out of my life." Another youth in his teens went to bed the first night at the camp with rocks hidden under his pillow. He had lived so surrounded by violence and threats against his life that he was frightened to be without a weapon in the middle of the night. Christian youth working in Operation Headstart have incredulously watched children drink their first glass of milk. A world of comfort, hope, and knowledge was unknown to them.

To work with underprivileged children and adults requires patience, courage, and special skills. A wholly fresh way of looking at things is necessary. Some of the poor are so subdued by their physical isolation and inability to communicate that they feel virtually abandoned. While adult realism is certainly important in the War on Poverty programs, the youthful volunteers in VISTA and other anti-poverty programs have the kinds of idealism and insights which can break through the alienation of poor children and adults.

For the same reasons Christian young people have found a keen sense of identification with the Peace Corps. Realism coupled with commitment spells the gratifying results which the Peace Corps has obtained. Spread through myriad cultures, languages, and needs, the volunteers have found their own lives enriched more even than they have been able to enrich the nations to which they have been sent. One volunteer said that what had begun for him as a rather bookish interest in comparative cultures had become a genuine involvement in the other culture. Each new insight did not merely add to his store of knowledge, but carried the power of giving pain or pleasure.

He went on to say that no real intellectual understanding can exist without a sense of identification at some deeper level. It is this sense of identification in which one's body, spirit, and talents are involved that makes life meaningful.

The Peace Corps has been involved on a wide scale with programs which include everything from a fisheries project in Togo to educational television in Colombia. The projects and the talents needed run the gamut of public health, sanitation, geology, coaching, construction, architecture, mechanics, forestry, and credit cooperatives.

One fairly new but fast developing area of involvement is the community development program. Peace Corps volunteers have the opportunity to live in small villages and towns and seek to help the townspeople develop political structures, educational institutions, credit and farm cooperatives, and new social structures. Actually such community development borders on genuine revolution.

It is little wonder that many of the returned Peace Corps volunteers find themselves eager to plunge into similar tasks in the United States. Many are consumed with restlessness. They are more objective in evaluating hometowns and local structures than they could have been otherwise. One volunteer who had returned from Latin America said, "I have found myself wanting to know all about my home city. I want to know what are the different groups, who runs the town, why have so many needed projects been left undone. Why are so many needy people overlooked?" He and a host of others like him are the catalysts who will bring change to our own land where it is needed.

Numerous lay organizations are attempting to meet urgent

needs throughout the world. An exemplary group is Lay-men's Overseas Service. This interdenominational move-ment based in Jackson, Mississippi, decided to find out what would happen when people decided to "give themselves away" for the sake of others. The results have been remark-able. Depending on the vocational need and the qualifica-tions of the volunteers, individuals participate for terms of service of two to twelve months in places all over the world. Physicians, dentists, commercial teachers, photo-journalists, secretaries, literacy specialists, recreational leaders and coaches, agricultural personnel, and music teachers have been involved overseas. Serving humanity in the name of Christ through such organizations has a revolutionary effect upon the volunteers. They become infected by a sense of urgency, challenge, and involvement. It would be difficult to chronicle the contributions of such volunteers who have committed their skills and their time to change their world.

What Is Your Motivation?

Motivation for such commitment of life is exceptionally important. Some people are motivated merely by sentimen-talism or a romantic urge for adventure. The Christian's motivation for service must be more than winning friends for the American way of life. He must have more than the desire to transplant his own culture overseas or to superim-pose his ideals and morality on people in another framework or community. The involvement of his life in the lives of others ought to go deeper than a mere anti-Communist struggle also. Thoughtful leaders remind us that communism would exult in seeing the Christian church fail to be the church and become instead an anti-Communist society. Motivation for Christian service is rooted in the nature of God, in the distress of the world, in the need of man, and in the fact that God in Christ is at work in the world and bids us join with him in what is already transpiring.

In overseas ministries and work, motivation is a key to success or failure. Kenneth Thompson reminds, "The United States, thrust suddenly onto the throne of world leadership, is both fortified and beset by its reforming zeal. Developments in other less favored countries yield slowly and often imperceptibly to our prompting and aid. Governments and societies in other lands are like plants; we are not their maker. Like a gardener we can patiently nurture them, tend and improve the soil, and pray for the grace of kindlier elements. But bursts of good intentions that light up the sky with impassioned exhortations to others to be as we are must remain as futile as the cries of the millennialist calling to God from the mountain top to come down and claim his own. Christians today must continually combat the temptation to believe that both God and man can be beguiled. . . . The world needs partners far more than patrons."

OPPORTUNITIES AND PROBLEMS

In international service the opportunities are limitless. From the Peace Corps to the State Department to private foundations to the United Nations to overseas business and teaching opportunities, there are places either on a short-term or a long-term basis for people in almost every vocation. If you are willing to be involved in another land as it makes history, the possibilities are as large as the globe itself.

The disparity in wealth between the average American overseas and the people with whom he works complicates the difficult problem of human relations between different cultures. The Peace Corps volunteers have helped to overcome the disparity by living at levels near the majority of the people in the nations where they work.

On the whole, however, the problem is a realistic one for most Americans. The American's image of himself may be rather distorted. He can be made smug by the fact that he drives an automobile in a country where very few do. He may be in a place of administrative leadership over a large number of nationals. His home may be staffed by one or more servants. He is tempted to be cliquish and class-conscious by relating socially only to other Americans or to a highly selected group of English-speaking nationals of wealth and culture.

For these and many more reasons, whether the American be a missionary, a government official, or a businessman overseas, his motivation, preparation, and willingness to share on an equalitarian level are of paramount importance. The future of international relations and the health of the nations to which Americans go to work and to minister are involved.

We live in such a highly interdependent world that all occupations ultimately touch international relations. Many occupations which will never take a person outside his own country significantly touch other parts of the world. A sense of perspective larger than the township mind thus becomes important. In our shrinking world, journalists, teachers, ministers, legislators, and many others have an opportunity to influence people toward a broader outlook. To foment peace with justice as an important goal will take a lifetime of creative thought and work on the part of many willing to pay the price. Others committed to the study of languages, economics, and politics are needed to stretch the minds of Americans who have too long been satisfied with local matters.

A shift in job emphasis might also make sharing one's faith a more significant involvement in human affairs. For example, a schoolteacher might decide to teach among the

foreign-born or in an underprivileged community. A shift of
location might also be involved, taking the teacher among
migrant workers or Indian settlements in the Southwest of
the United States. A typist might decide to work for a reform
organization or in the offices of a civil rights organization. A
skilled business administrator might decide to use his talents
in institutions and programs emerging among the poor, the
mentally ill, or in educational institutions which have suffered from inadequate staff. The possibilities of a shift in
emphasis are without limit. Once again the price is involvement. Less dollars, less security, and less luxury may be a
part of the price. Along with involvement, of course, may
come more meaningful personal fulfillment.

Within the scope of the anti-poverty programs being
pressed by government, private foundations, and church
groups, there are also tremendous opportunities for job commitment as well as for voluntary service. Among the most
important programs being developed in the nation are the
community action programs. These vary from place to place
as the needs of the people vary in different sectors of the
nation. The efforts must be part of the overall goal to help
people escape poverty, rather than simply to make poverty
more bearable. Listed are some illustrations which might
be part of a community action program and in which you
might find involvement:

1. Providing special and remedial education with particular emphasis on reading, writing, and mathematics.
2. Providing academic counseling and guidance services
   and school social work services.
3. Providing after-school study centers, tutoring, and sum-
   mer weekend and after-school classes.
4. Establishing programs for the benefit of preschool
   children.

5. Reducing adult illiteracy.
6. Developing and carrying out special education or other programs for migrant and other transient families.
7. Improving the living conditions of the elderly.
8. Arranging for or providing health examinations and health education for school children in underprivileged sectors.
9. Rehabilitating and retraining of physically and mentally handicapped persons.
10. Providing health, rehabilitation, employment, educational, and related services to young men not qualified for military service.
11. Providing community child care centers and youth activity centers.
12. Improving housing and living facilities and home management skills.
13. Providing services to enable families from rural areas to meet the new problems of urban living.
14. Providing recreational and physical fitness services and facilities.

Obviously there is opportunity for many lifetimes of service and also for voluntary part-time involvement in such possibilities.

One of the key persons emerging in American life today is the community organizer. In slums, racially changing neighborhoods, and among many minority groups he is an important figure for change. Many Christians who are committed to responsible social change should prepare for the challenge of such a difficult job. The community organizer digs into the resignation and hopelessness of people and helps them to articulate their needs and desires. He is a catalytic agent reminding people, "There *is* something you can do about it!" Because of his skills in psychology, economics, and politics, he is able to move persons and groups from dormant hostility to giving vent to their problem or problems.

Otherwise, the submerged frustration of groups within our nation may become a volcanic force eventually erupting in vindictive hate. The task of a community organizer requires self-discipline, integrity, and patience. He must command respect in order to have a hearing. He must know himself inside and out and act like the self he knows he is. Courageous and prepared Christians motivated by love and justice would be invaluable in the role of community organizer. Here is another place where the price to pay for service and fulfillment is involvement.

The new opportunities of service to bring freedom to all men are exciting. For the first time on a large scale, Christians may give themselves vocationally to the task of awakening man to fulfillment and dignity in life. Free enterprise in ideas is a contemporary frontier of service. People cannot long work under conditions which are fixed by leaders afraid of ideas.

Today's Christian may find his vocational and geographical location shifting rapidly in attempting to meet the ever-changing needs of society. You may be called on to arm men with logic, evidence, and ability to analyze and to distinguish between facts and fiction. Neither slogans nor quick solutions can remedy many of the deep social and political problems of our nation.

Willingness to cast your life in the midst of these problems for their solution is the price you must be willing to pay. Your Christian zeal, intelligence, and preparation may lead you toward political service at the local or the national level. The old concept "politics is dirty" must give way to a sense of responsible participation. You will need intelligence and analysis, a sensitivity to the reality of power, acceptance of controversy as normative, and a recognition of the necessity of broad action to eliminate grievances.

No establishment, whether political, religious, or cultural, ever welcomes agents of change. You must seize the opportunity to speak, to act, and to bring about needed change.

Our society tends to place undue emphasis on salvation through technology. While the scientific community may guarantee hope in many areas, there will continue to be need for vast change in family and social structures and in the establishment of worthy values. Neither human need nor technology is static. What we must save ourselves from is an aimless tomorrow. The human resources industries are going to require more people all the time. Retraining and new vocation insights thus become important. Status and caste concepts of work must be exploded. The handful of vocations once considered as elite must give way to broad cross examination of vocation in order to meet the needs and opportunities of the new age. It is not our resources that are lacking at this time, but rather our will to use them. Our wisdom and our ability must be employed to rise to the possibilities that science and technology have placed in our hands. Man must not be lost in the process. It is to transforming him and his world that we are dedicated.

In such a complexity of need and vocation, your response may only be boredom, unconcern, fatigue, or evasion. After the beheading of Sir Thomas More in Robert Bolt's play *A Man For All Seasons*, Common Man comes to the center of the stage, having taken off his mask and says: "I'm breathing. . . . Are you breathing too? . . . It's nice, isn't it? It isn't difficult to keep alive, friends—just don't make trouble—or if you must make trouble, make the sort of trouble that is expected. Well, I don't need to tell you that. . . ."

But this is precisely the price of discipleship: to make trouble, to raise questions, to effect change, to transform your world. A student from India raised the question of whether or not we American Christians are willing to pay the price. He reminded that it was the American democratic revolution which had spread ideas of political and social revolution over the whole world. Yet today, when this contagious revolution moves through once-dormant or -colonial nations, Americans tend to become cautious, anxious, and ultraconservative in response. The Indian student said, "When your own politics, or economic self-preservation become endangered, you tend to be against change and revolution in other nations in spite of the fact that you once sparked the ideas which touched off the revolution which now consumes old structures and produces new ones in our nations." His charge hits us where we live.

CHRISTIAN ACTION WHERE NEED IS THE GREATEST

Christian action must be directed to the situation where the need is the greatest. So too must your life in genuine discipleship. No Christian has the right to avoid a dirty situation which might soil or wound. The cost of discipleship is involvement in life for the redemption of life, whatever the circumstances or the consequences. It may keep you at home or it may send you far away. But it *will* heighten your awareness of others, your sense of justice, and the commitment of what you are and have.

En route to negotiate a cease-fire between Katanga and the United Nations forces, Dag Hammarskjöld died in a fiery plane crash near Ndola, Northern Rhodesia. The scholarly mystical Christian had been the United Nations' Secretary General for eight years. Only two months before his death, he had written in his diary:

>Tired
>And lonely,
>So tired
>The heart aches.
>Meltwater trickles
>Down the rocks,
>The fingers are numb,
>The knees tremble.
>It is now,
>Now, that you must not give in.
>
>On the path of the others
>Are resting places,
>Places in the sun
>Where they can meet.
>But this
>Is your path,
>And it is now,
>Now, that you must not fail.
>
>Weep
>If you can,
>Weep,
>But do not complain.
>The way chose you—
>And you must be thankful.

The whole world was his concern. Of it and himself, he had said, "In our era the road to holiness necessarily passes through the world of action."

The price of true living? Involvement!

References

CHAPTER ONE–IS IT WORTH YOUR LIFE?

"American Idealism, 1965," *Saturday Review* (June 26, 1965), p. 14.

Bayne, Stephen F. *Christian Living* (New York: Seabury Press, 1957), pp. 137, 140.

Eliot, T. S. "Burnt Norton," *Four Quartets* (New York: Harcourt, Brace & Co., 1943).

Feiffer, Jules. Cartoon, *New Republic* (January 22, 1966), p. 27.

Janusch, John Buettner. In *The Chapel Hill*, Chapel Hill, N. C. (October 6, 1965).

Koestler, Arthur. *Darkness at Noon* (New York: Modern Library). *Newsweek* (March 30, 1964), p. 68.

West, Charles. *Outside the Camp* (New York: Doubleday & Co., 1959), p. 77.

CHAPTER TWO–KEY TO THE AUTHENTIC: TRUTH

Benedict, Ruth. *Patterns of Culture* (New York: Houghton Mifflin Co., 1934), pp. 2–3.

Berger, Peter. *The Noise of Solemn Assemblies* (New York: Doubleday & Co., 1961), p. 126.

Edwards, David L. *The Honest to God Debate* (Philadelphia: Westminster Press, 1963), p. 40.

Harkness, Georgia. *Understanding the Christian Faith* (Nashville: Abingdon Press, 1952), pp. 21–22, 66.

McGinley, Phyllis. "The Day After Sunday," from *Times Three* (New York: Viking Press, 1961), p. 4.

Stringfellow, William. *Dissenter in a Great Society* (New York: Holt, Rinehart & Winston, 1966), pp. 129–30.

Temple, William. *Nature, Man and God* (London: Macmillan & Co., 1951), pp. 19–20.

Tillich, Paul. *The Shaking of the Foundations* (New York: Charles Scribner's Sons, 1948), p. 117.

CHAPTER THREE—
DISCOVERING THE REAL YOU: REPENTANCE

Boyd, Malcolm. *Are You Running With Me Jesus?* (New York: Holt, Rinehart & Winston, 1965), p. 119.

Niebuhr, Reinhold. *An Interpretation of Christian Ethics* (Living Age Books; New York: Meridian Books, 1956), p. 201.

Tillich, Paul. *The New Being* (New York: Charles Scribner's Sons, 1955), p. 11.

Tillich, Paul. *The Shaking of the Foundations* (New York: Charles Scribner's Sons, 1948), pp. 158–59.

CHAPTER FOUR—
BETTER THAN WHISTLING IN THE DARK: COURAGE

Anderson, Robert. From "First of the Month" column by Cleveland Amory, *Saturday Review* (July 4, 1964).

Baldwin, James. *The Fire Next Time* (New York: Dial Press, 1964), p. 23.

Cox, Harvey. *The Secular City* (New York: Macmillan Co., 1965), pp. 125–48.

Frankl, Viktor. *Man's Search For Meaning* (Boston: Beacon Press, 1963), pp. 14, 78.

Gregory, Dick. *Nigger* (New York: E. P. Dutton & Co., 1964), p. 224.

Howe, Reuel L. *The Miracle of Dialogue* (New York: Seabury Press, 1963), p. 126.

Tillich, Paul. *The Courage To Be* (New Haven: Yale University Press, 1952), p. 3.

Yevtushenko, Yevgeny. "Talk," from *Selected Poems,* trans. Robin Milner-Gulland and Peter Levi (Baltimore: Penguin Books, 1962), p. 81.

CHAPTER FIVE—LOVE IN ACTION: JUSTICE

Bagdikian, Ben. *In the Midst of Plenty* (Boston: Beacon Press, 1964), p. 191.

Bennett, John C. "The Church and Power Conflicts," *Christianity and Crisis* (March 22, 1965), pp. 47, 48.

Bonhoeffer, Dietrich. *Cost of Discipleship* (New York: Macmillan Co., 1959), p. 133.

Cox, Harvey. *The Secular City* (New York: Macmillan Co., 1965), p. 134.

Gibran, Kahlil. *Spirits Rebellious* (New York: Alfred A. Knopf, 1948), pp. 65, 67.

Haselden, Kyle. *The Racial Problem in Christian Perspective* (New York: Harper & Bros., 1959), pp. 176–77.

Mayer, Milton. *What Can A Man Do?* (Chicago: University of Chicago Press, 1964), p. 40.

Smallzried, Kay. *Spilled Milk; Litanies for Living* (New York: Oxford University Press, 1964), p. 37.

Tillich, Paul. *Love, Power and Justice* (New York: Oxford University Press, 1954)), p. 84.

Tolstoy, Leo. Quoted by Davis, J., and Hester, H. B. *On the Brink* (New York: Lyle Stuart, 1959), p. 89.

Unamuno, Miguel de. *The Tragic Sense of Life,* trans. J. E. Crawford Flitch (London: Macmillan & Co., 1921; R.E.P.R. London: William Collins Sons & Co. [Fontana Library Edition], 1962), p. 21.

van der Post, Laurens. *The Dark Eye in Africa* (New York: William Morrow & Co., 1955), pp. 214, 215.

CHAPTER SIX—A WAY OF LIFE: MORALITY

Beach, Waldo. *Conscience on Campus* (New York: Association Press, 1958), pp. 13–14, 117.

Cox, Harvey. *The Secular City* (New York: Macmillan Co., 1965), pp. 192–217.

Ellul, Jacques. *The Technological Society* (New York: Harcourt, Brace & World, 1964), p. 432.

Guardini, Romano. *Power and Responsibility,* trans. Elinor C. Briefs (Chicago: Henry Regnery Co., 1961), pp. XII, XIII.

Rowland, Stanley J., Jr. *Ethics, Crime and Redemption* (Philadelphia: Westminster Press, 1963), p. 55.

Tawney, R. H. *Religion and the Rise of Capitalism* (New York: Harcourt, Brace & Co., 1926), p. 211.

CHAPTER SEVEN—THE PRICE TO PAY: INVOLVEMENT

Bolt, Robert. *A Man For All Seasons* (New York: Random House, 1962), pp. 162–63.

Bonhoeffer, Dietrich. *Prisoner for God: Letters and Papers from Prison,* ed. Eberhard Bethge, trans. Reginald H. Fuller (New York: Macmillan Co., 1953), pp. 168–69.

Camus, Albert. *The Fall,* trans. Justin O'Brien (New York: Alfred A. Knopf, 1959), p. 147.

Dostoyevsky, Fyodor. *The Brothers Karamazov,* trans. Constance Garnett (New York: Modern Library, 1945), p. 64.

Hammarskjöld, Dag. *Markings* (New York: Alfred A. Knopf, 1965), pp. 122, 213.

Oldham, J. H. *Life is Commitment* (London: S.C.M. Press, 1953), p. 24.

Thompson, Kenneth. *Christian Ethics and the Dilemmas of Foreign Policy* (Durham, N.C.: Duke University Press, 1959), p. 129.